# WINTER NIGHT

# WINTER NIGHT

## SELECTED POEMS OF
# Attila József

TRANSLATED FROM THE HUNGARIAN
# BY JOHN BÁTKI

FIELD TRANSLATION SERIES 23

OBERLIN COLLEGE PRESS
Oberlin, Ohio

Some of these translations first appeared, in earlier versions, in the following magazines: *The Baltimore Sun, Choice, Collegium Budapest Bulletin, December, Exquisite Corpse, FIELD, The Greenfield Review, The Iowa Review, The Lamp in the Spine, Mundus Artium, Maelstrom, New Directions 24, The Nickel Review, Poetry, The Seneca Review, South Dakota Review, Southern Poetry Review, Talisman, The World.*

Library of Congress Cataloging-in-Publication Data

József, Attila (translations and introduction by John Bátki)
    Winter Night: Selected Poems
    (The FIELD Translation Series v. 23)


LC: 97-066615
ISBN: 0-932440-78-9 (pbk.)

# Contents

# Translator's Introduction

"Your winter night . . . all merciless and hopeless, the one that kills you in the end, the one that has no consideration of any human pith or earthly significance except to destroy all of us completely. . . . It's impossible to love in the middle of so much icy night and unhappiness."

Jack Kerouac: *The Town and the City*

The winter night Jack Kerouac refers to in his first novel is a North American version of the one Attila József charted and surveyed "like an owner/his property" in his 1933 poem. The coincidence signals a deeper kinship, kindred sensibilities and sensitivities: both poets are preoccupied with the pain and sadness of existence, both are ever mindful of emptiness. Kerouac's is a more consciously Buddhist attitude than József's—although in the 1934 poem "Village" the Hungarian poet sees "emerald Buddhas in the dewy grass" (thus granting toads the Buddhahood denied them by the Zen saying). Farther down the road, Allen Ginsberg in his 1986 poem "Cosmopolitan Greetings" not only borrows a phrase ("molecules clanking against each other") but in a note graciously credits the source, Attila József. Indeed, József appears in another Ginsberg poem. "May Days 1988" names Attila József [sic] as one of the "80 volumes behind the headboard for browsing." The book referred to is my long out-of-print *Attila József's Poems and Texts*, published in Iowa City in 1976.

Allen Ginsberg, to whose memory I offer this writing, generously promised an Introduction to *Winter Night*, and had the manuscript by his bedside during the final weeks of his life. So now the bereaved inheritor of this task can only go back to the title poem of *Cosmopolitan Greetings* and search for clues:

Stand up against governments, against God.

And I hear Attila József answering, in his youthful poem, "With a Pure Heart":

I am fatherless, motherless,
godless and countryless . . .

Allen Ginsberg:

     Ordinary mind includes eternal perceptions.

Attila József:

     Dusk fondles a slim young locust tree.
                      ("Village")
     In the abandoned factory yard
     a hardy dandelion opens a parasol.
                      ("Elegy")

Allen Ginsberg:

     Catch yourself thinking.

Attila József:

     For a whole week now, over and over,
     I've been thinking only of mother.
                      ("Mama")

Allen Ginsberg:

     Remember the future.

Attila Józscf:

     Words used by the poet, trusting
     in future times' care.
                      ("Village")

Allen Ginsberg:

     Two molecules clanking against each
        other require an observer to become
        scientific data.

Attila József:

     . . . Bone, can you hear the silence?
     Molecule clinks against molecule.
                      ("Winter Night")

Allen Ginsberg:

     Inside skull vast as outside skull.
     Mind is outer space.

Attila József:

> My soul is empty. It would fly
> up to the great mother Emptiness.
>
> ("The Poet and His Times")

And so on. The parallels are endless. I believe Allen would have welcomed Attila in the language of the bardic tradition, the language and tradition of William Blake, Emily Dickinson, Walt Whitman, Jack Kerouac.

*

A few words about these translations. Working and reworking them in the course of more than two decades I have come to realize my limits. My versions, I trust, err on the side of overfaithfulness to the literal meaning and form of the originals. At best, they will suggest some of the formal qualities and much of the light and dark that emanates from József's poetry. Wherever possible, I tried to follow the syllable count and rhyme scheme of József's lines. In one or two instances of poems I have heard set to music ("Pearl," "Mysteries") I tried to produce lyrics singable to the same tunes. I am very much aware that my versions remain translations —they cannot possess the transparent clarity, the lean energy of József's idiom. Still, let them be a part of the ongoing apocatastasis that we, surviving humans of the twentieth century's Winter Night, offer to makers of the future.

*John Bátki*
*Syracuse, New York*
*4 May 1997*

# Attila József: CURRICULUM VITAE
## (February 1937)

I was born in Budapest in 1905, and am Greek Orthodox by religion. My father, the late Áron József, left the country when I was three years old, and I was sent to live with foster parents at Öcsöd through the agency of the League for the Protection of Children. I lived there until I was seven, and even started working as a swineherd, like most of the poor children in the village. When I was seven years old my mother, the late Borbála Pöcze, brought me back to Budapest and enrolled me in the second grade of elementary school. My mother supported us—myself and my two sisters—by doing washing and house-cleaning. She worked at different homes and was away all day. Without parental supervision I skipped school and played in the streets. In the third-grade reader, however, I found some interesting stories about King Attila and I became a voracious reader. These stories about the King of the Huns interested me not only because my name happened to be Attila but also because my foster parents at Öcsöd had insisted on calling me "Steve." After consulting the neighbors they came to the conclusion, in front of me, that there was no such name as Attila. I was stunned; I felt that they cast doubt on my very existence. I believe that my discovery of the tales about Attila the Hun had a decisive influence on all my ambitions from then on; in the final analysis this is what might have led me to literature. This experience turned me into a thinking person, one who listens to the opinions of others, but examines them critically in his own mind; someone who resigns himself to being called "Steve" until one day he is justified in his belief that his name is Attila, as he had known all along.

The World War broke out when I was nine, and our lot became progressively worse. I did my share of standing in lines: there were times when I stepped into the line in front of a food store at nine in the evening, only to be told, when my turn came at eight in the morning, that the cooking lard was all gone. I helped my mother as well as I could. I sold drinking water at the Világ movie theater. I stole firewood and coal from the Ferencváros freight station so that we would have fuel for our stove. I made colorful paper pin-wheels and peddled them to children who were better off than I, carried shopping bags and packages from the Market Hall, and so on. In the summer of 1918 I was taken for a holiday in Dalmatia by the King Charles Children's Fund. My mother by this time was seriously ill with a uterine tumor, and I had to apply on my own for assistance from the League for the Protection of Children. For a brief period I was sent to Monor. On my return to Budapest I sold news-papers and trafficked at first in postage stamps, then in the blue and white inflationary banknotes. During the Roman-ian occupation I worked as a breadboy at the Café Emke. Meanwhile, having finished the five grades of elementary school, I was attending secondary school.

My mother died at Christmastime, 1919. The Orphans' Board appointed my brother-in-law, Dr. Ödön Makai, now deceased, to be my guardian. Through one spring and sum-mer I served on the tugboats Storm, Turk and Tatar of the Atlantica Ocean Shipping Co. At this time I took the exams of the fourth grade of secondary school, as a private stu-dent. Then my guardian and Dr. Sándor Geisswein sent me to train as a novice with the Salesian Order at Nyergesuj-falu. I spent only two weeks there, since I am Greek Ortho-dox and not Roman Catholic. From here I went to the Demke boarding school at Makó, where I soon obtained free tuition. In the summer I tutored at Mezöhegyes to earn my room and board. I finished the sixth year of high school with excellent grades, despite the fact that, lacking then as before the guidance of a good friend, I had several times attempted suicide. My first poems appeared at this time: *Nyugat* pub-lished some of my poems written at the age of 17. They took me for a child prodigy; actually I was merely an orphan.

After the sixth year of high school I dropped out because I was lonely and had nothing to do. I did not have to study be-cause I would learn the lessons after hearing the teacher's lectures in class—as my good grades attested. I worked in the village of Kiszombor as a crop watchman and field hand, then did some tutoring. At the urging of two of my kind teachers, I decided to take my final exams for the graduation diploma. I took the exams on the last two years' material combined, and managed to graduate a year ahead of my classmates. However, as I had only three months to prepare,

I received a "good" in the seventh, and only a "satisfactory" in the eighth-year exam. It was about this time that I was prosecuted for blasphemy in one of my published poems. The High Court acquitted me.

After that I was a book salesman in Budapest. Then, during the time of the inflation, I worked in an office of the Mauthner private bank. After the introduction of the Hintz system I was transferred to the accounting department, and shortly after this, much to the annoyance of my senior colleagues, I was entrusted with supervising the currency values on accounts days. My enthusiasm was somewhat dampened by the fact that, in addition to my own work, I was often stuck with duties that belonged to my senior colleagues. Nor did they fail to chaff me about the poems that were appearing in periodicals. "I also used to write poems at your age," was the typical comment. Later the bank failed.

I decided once and for all that I would be a writer and that I would find some employment closely connected with literature. I enrolled in the School of Liberal Arts at the University of Szeged to study French and Hungarian literature, and Philosophy. I took 52 hours of lectures and seminars a week, 20 hours of which were for my end-semester examinations, which I passed with distinction. I ate at different friends' homes on different days and paid my rent out of royalties for my poems. I was very proud when Professor Lajos Dézsi declared me qualified to undertake independent research. However, all my hopes were dashed when Professor Antal Horger, my examiner in Hungarian Philology, called me in and, in the presence of two witnesses—I still remember their names, both are teachers at this time—declared that as long as he was around I would never be a secondary school teacher, because, as he said, "the kind of person who writes this sort of poem"—and here he held up a copy of the periodical *Szeged*—"is not to be trusted with the education of the future generation." People often talk about the irony of fate: this poem of mine, "With a Pure Heart," became quite famous; seven articles have been written about it; Lajos Hatvany more than once described it as a document of the post-war generation for "future ages"; Ignotus, writing in *Nyugat*, said that he had "cradled and caressed this beautiful poem in his soul, murmured it and hummed it," and in his "Ars Poetica" he picked this poem as a model exhibit of modern poetry.

The next year, at the age of twenty, I went to Vienna where I enrolled at the University. I made my living selling newspapers outside the Rathaus Keller restaurant and working as janitor at the Collegium Hungaricum. The director, Antal Lábán, put an end to this when he heard about me, and started giving me free meals at the Collegium; he also found me students to tutor. I tutored the two sons of Zoltán Hajdu, managing director of the Anglo-Austrian Bank. From the frightful slum in Vienna where for four months I did not even have any bedsheets I went straight to Hatvan as the guest of the Hatvany family at their mansion. Then the lady of the house, Mrs. Albert Hirsch, paid my travel expenses to Paris at the end of the summer. There I enrolled at the Sorbonne. I spent the following summer at the seaside in a fishing village in the south of France.

After that I returned to Budapest, where I attended two semesters at the University. I did not take my teacher's diploma since, in view of Antal Horger's threat, I knew that I would not be able to obtain a position. Then when the Foreign Trade Institute was founded I was given employment there as French correspondent. (I believe my former manager, Mr. Sándor Kóródi, would be quite willing to provide a reference.) At this time I was overtaken by a series of unexpected blows that, toughened by life as I was, still left me unable to go on. The National Health Service first sent me to a sanatorium; afterwards I was recommended for National Assistance because of severe depression. I left my job because I realized that I could not stay on as a burden at a young institution. Since then I have been living on my writing. I am the editor of *Szép Szó*, a periodical of literature and criticism. Apart from my native language, Hungarian, I read and write French and German, I am experienced in Hungarian and French business correspondence, and am a good typist. I have studied shorthand and with a month's practice would regain my speed. I am familiar with the technicalities of printing and can express myself clearly and precisely. I consider myself honest and believe I am an intelligent and hard worker.

---

Translator's Note: In the last year of his life József considered applying for a job at a bank, where he was required to write this C.V.

# Chronology

1905 Born in Budapest on April 11, the third child (after sisters Jolán and Etel) of the factory worker Áron József and the domestic worker/ washerwoman Borbála Pöcze.

1908 Father abandons family.

1910-12 With foster parents at village of Öcsöd.

1917-18 At Monor orphanage.

1918 Sister Jolán marries the lawyer Ödön Makai, who two years later becomes Attila's legal guardian.

1919 Mother dies of cancer on December 27, while Attila is visiting grandparents in the country.

1920 Enters boarding school at Makó.

1922 First volume of poems: *Szépség koldusa* [*Beggar of Beauty*].

1923 Drops out of school; takes private graduation exams.

1924 Trial for alleged "blasphemy" of his poem "Rebellious Christ." Matriculates at Szeged University, studies literature and philosophy.

1925 Second volume of poems: *Nem én kiáltok* [*That's Not Me Shouting*]. Leaves university after being "advised away" by Professor Horger, who was outraged by the publication of the poem "With a Pure Heart."

September: off to Vienna with two suitcases (one full of manuscripts), a loaf of bread, a stick of salami and 30 schillings. Signs up for courses at the university. Meets the literary patron Baron Hatvany and the poet/painter Kassák, editor of the periodical *MA*.

1926 Vienna. From a letter to his sister: "Anna Lesznai, Béla Balázs and Georg Lukács (especially the latter) all consider me a truly great poet, the first proletarian lyricist possessing international (not cosmopolitan!) qualities—a poet who is destined to receive at the earliest opportunity your (preferably) sizeable remittance."

September: arrives in Paris, enrolls at the Sorbonne.

| 1927 | The cover of *L'Esprit Nouveau*, No. 1: "hans arp, willi baumeister, marcel breuer, paul dermee, walter gropius, attila józsef, fernand leger, moholy-nagy, piet mondrian, f.t. marinetti, kurt schwitters, tristan tzara, *et al.*" Summer: at Cagnes-sur-Mer. |
|---|---|
| 1927-8 | Two semesters at the University of Budapest. From a National Student Relief Fund application form: "I have worked as tutor, newspaper vendor, ship's boy, street paver, bookkeeper, bank clerk, book salesman, paper boy, stenographer, typist, watchman in a cornfield, poet, translator, critic, delivery boy, busboy, stevedore, construction worker, day laborer." Love affair with Márta Vágó, whose family sends her to study at the London School of Economics. Hospitalized for the first time ("nervous breakdown"). |
| 1929 | Third volume of poems: *Nincsen apám, se anyám [Fatherless and Motherless].* One hundred copies were passed by the author directly into the hands of the public, on the street. |
| 1930 | Joins illegal Communist Party. Judit Szántó becomes his companion (until 1936). |
| 1931 | His fourth volume, *Döntsd a tökét, ne siránkozz! [Strike at Capital, Instead of Wailing]* (poems and Villon-translations), is confiscated and the author is prosecuted on charges of "political agitation and obscenity." Begins psychoanalytic treatment. |
| 1932 | His fifth volume, *Külvárosi éj [Night in the Slums].* |
| 1933 | Expelled from Communist Party. |
| 1934 | Sixth volume: *Medvetánc [Bear Dance]* (new and selected poems). |
| 1935 | Hospitalized for second time, for severe depression. |
| 1936 | Becomes co-editor, along with Pál Ignotus, of *Szép Szó*, a literary periodical financed by Baron Hatvany. In December, he meets "Flora," the final great love. Publication of his last volume of poems, *Nagyon fáj [It Hurts a Lot].* |

1937      January: meets Thomas Mann. Police interference prevents József from public reading of his poem welcoming Mann.

February: writes "Curriculum Vitae" as part of projected job application.

Notebook entry on his birthday: "Thirty-two years ago—more precisely, at 9 P.M. on April 11, 1905, according to the penitentiary records —after a judiciary detention of nine months I was sentenced to lifelong correction in a workhouse, on counts of sedition, espionage, betrayal of secrets, indecent exposure, vagrancy, repeated scandalous behavior and pathological prevarication. My appeal for pardon having been rejected, I was transferred into the world of incorrigible criminals. The authorities concealed the ineffectualness of the investigation by presenting evidence obtained under torture which, I can testify, lasted an eternity. I maintained my innocence in vain; the court accepted the results of the investigation, and my forced confession, as the basis of its decision."

Summer: after a breakdown, admitted to the Szieszta Sanatorium, where he is subjected to drastic psychopharmaceutical therapy, including insulin shock treatment.

November 4: Discharged in care of his two sisters, who take him to Balatonszárszó, where he dies on December 3, a suicide, under the wheels of freight train 1284.

## A Tired Man

Solemn peasants in the fields
straggle homeward without a word.
Side by side we lie, the river and I,
fresh grasses slumber under my heart.

A deep calm is rolling in the river.
My heavy cares are now as light as dew.
I'm not man, or child, "Hungarian" or "brother"—
lying here is just a tired man, like you.

Evening ladles out the quiet,
I'm a warm slice from its loaf of bread.
In the peaceful sky the stars come out
to sit on the river and shine on my head.

# GLASSMAKERS

Glassmakers light huge fires
and stir their blood and sweat
into the materials
that boil transparent
in their crucibles.
Then, with what's left of their strength,
they pour the glass into plates
and roll it completely smooth.

And when the sun comes up
they carry light to the cities
and to the smallest village huts.

Sometimes they are called laborers,
at other times, poets—
though one is as good as the other.
Slowly they run out of blood
and grow transparent:
large crystal windows to the future
built on you.

## DIAMOND

There is always a time for psalms.

We stand on a diamond mountain,
but our pockets are filled with pebbles.
We have long forgotten the angels we were,
and stuffed our white wings into fat cushions.
Prayers thirst for our strength now
and the flagstones would wear out under our knees.
The star in our hearts is frozen.

Yes, yes, that's right.
The marines all sank to the bottom.
Now peaceful ferrymen are sailing toward God.
Even the oldest of men
sit down on plain benches prior to chores
and preach patience
to the faraway fish of transience.

Yes, that's right.
So let's not believe now, my friends,
that instead of throwing balls
we used to throw our fists!
We must caress everything,
even the hyenas and toads.

We stand on a diamond mountain.
Severe snow, cover our sins,
loosen our tongues, heavenly light!

O you infinite crystal!

## 1924

## AND WE KEEP LOOKING FOR JUSTICE

So our legs wear down to stumps,
hey-ho, we whistle, and plod on
looking for justice, even though
it's nowhere to be found till now.

We lug our brains instead of packs,
so many Abels fingering the axe,
none ask if our hearts are dead,
so our thoughts are devil-fed,
yet our souls are driven by God,
the whip cracks, we plow hard.

Wintertime's our shivering time,
who cares, we'd be feeling fine
but our eyes and ears freeze like birds,
to thaw them out takes fevered words,
we don't sleep in the summer shade,
our pockets are full of promises made,
we stand, masters of our own fate,
always winning, even in defeat,
nothing beats us, no woman or hunger,
north or south, where to, we wonder,
and slap hands with every beggar,
we're at home in the worst weather,
our clasped hands have fused together,
still we don't pray, or sin, either,
we may starve but we won't hunger,
each time we arrive earlier,
the future tramples on our mouth,
a more decent world! we shout,
love, and freedom, are what we want,
our faces blessèd, feet wind-borne,
we seek the way through stone and thorn
where nobody has gone before,
hey-ho, our song gives good solace,
we lack tables but not words' grace —
and we keep looking for justice.

## DISABLED VETERANS

Along with their peasant legs
the shovels, too, have been cut off.
The warm rain of colors will never
relieve their eyes' drought.

Ringing bellstrokes
molten into satanic tanks
shattered with grenades
those slim obelisks, their backbones.

Through their pierced lungs
foaming terrors march groaning
and prison camps lie interned
in their tortured brains.

These are the men of whom
their mothers got back something,
across the toll of those
more merciful lime pits

where all sorts of stuttering Christs
are calcifying into one body
so that the orgy of death rattles grows
into one monstrous sermon on the mount.

The breadwinning hands
of their missing arms are clenched,
and aflame, ringing the bell
for peace in their hearts.

## FOR SEVEN DAYS

I dip my pen into ink,
I dip myself into the clear blue.

I tug at the bell ropes,
I beat my poor head against the wall.

Who can see the promised road
at the tip of our hanging tongues,
see that nothing is in vain, that all
was not lost through our slashed veins,
that even the rat aspires to be a crystal,
and the little crumb looks down on the lesser crumb,
that you can find yourself pure in others,
and calm exists in the inevitable rush,
that our breath could set buildings on fire,
while a sprinkle of water's supposed to appease us,
and bridges blow up inside the poor?

O my friends, for seven days I have not eaten.

## A JUST MAN

My eyes, you girls who milk the light,
turn over your pails,
tongue, you tall handsome whooping young man,
leave your day-labor,
jump out of me, beast, escape to Asia,
to the roots of sweating forests,
backbone, collapse under the Eiffel Tower,
nose, you sailing Greenland whaler,
keep your harpoon away from smells,
hands, make a pilgrimage to Rome,
legs, kick each other into a ditch,
ears, surrender
your drums, your drums!
Leap over to Australia, my thigh,
you rose-pink marsupial,
belly, you light balloon, soar
to Saturn, fly away!
Then shall I step out onto my lips,
with a curving shout jump into your ears,
and stopped clocks will tock again,
villages will shine like floodlights,
cities will be whitewashed,
and my vertebrae can scatter
in all directions of the wind,
for I will be standing tall
among the crooked bodies of the dead.

## THAT'S NOT ME SHOUTING

That's not me shouting, it's the earth that roars,
beware, beware, for Satan is raving,
better lie low deep in a clear stream,
flatten yourself into a pane of glass,
hide behind the light of diamonds,
among insects under stones,
go hide inside the fresh-baked bread,
you poor man, you poor man.
With the fresh rain seep into the ground,
it's useless to plunge into yourself
when only in others' eyes can you bathe your face.
Be the edge of a small blade of grass,
you'll be greater than the world's axis.
O machines, birds, leaves and stars!
Our barren mother is praying for a child.
My friend, my dear, beloved friend,
it may be horrible or splendid, but
that's not me shouting, it's the earth that roars.

## THE DOG

He was so shaggy, sloppy wet,
his coat a yellow flame,
his hunger-trimmed
desire-wasted
sad flanks
sent the cool night breeze
streaming a long way.
He ran and he begged.
Crowded, sighing churches
stood in his eyes
and he scavenged
for breadcrumbs, any old scrap.

I felt as sorry for him
as if that poor dog had
crawled out of myself.
I saw in him all
that is mangy in the world.

We go to bed because we have to,
because night puts us to bed,
and we fall asleep
because starvation lulls.
But before dropping off,
as we lie, like the city,
mute under the chill vault
of fatigue and clarity
suddenly he creeps forth
from his daytime hideout
inside us,
that oh so hungry,
muddy, ragged dog
hunting for
god-scraps,
god-crumbs.

## A Fine Summer Evening

It is a fine summer evening.

Rumbling trains arrive and depart,
frightened factories are wailing,
soot-black rooftops are blackened by evening,
newsboys clamor under the streetlights,
cars scuttle back and forth,
streetcars clang in a great procession,
neon signs scream that you are blind,
walls that trail off into side streets
wave their posters back at you.
Ahead of you, behind, everywhere,
poster-faced men are scurrying,
and beyond the big city blocks you can see
hallelujah-crying-howling-groaning-swearing
panting-coldly-cunningly-grasping
men
climbing a man-ladder,
and veins are swelling
on the necks of angry avenues.
You can hear the silent office drudge's shriek,
the slow footfalls of workers going home
as if they were old sages
with nothing left to do on earth.
You can hear the soft movements of the pickpocket's wrists,
and the peasant smacking his lips
as he lifts a broad strip of hay
from his neighbor's land.
I who am listening can hear it all.
The worm whimpers in the beggar's bones,
women nose about me,
but I have come from a long way off,
so I just sit on my friendly doorstep
and keep silent.

It is a fine summer evening.

# 1925

## WIND-RIDING BIRD

What now, beggarman, up in arms again?

> Oh, far from it, but my coat is torn.
> I would like another one
> less worn.

Did you by any chance drink up your paycheck?

> No sir, I'd never had no paycheck,
> never had no, still don't have no, paycheck.
> They call me and I'd work till red sundown,
> work the whole day long since the crack of red dawn,
> grandpa always told me I'd never see no paycheck.

Hey you bum, get away from here!

> Yes, I'm leaving this place, and crossing the ocean,
> and across the ocean, sail into fellow hearts,
> and from there, I'll fly into the hurricane's eye—
> let her sing if she must, hey, I can hear her cry
> loud and clear, wind-crying storm petrel on high.

## With A Pure Heart

I am fatherless, motherless,
godless and countryless,
have no cradle, no funeral shroud,
and no lover to kiss me proud.

For the third day I have had
no food, not a piece of bread.
My strength is my twenty years—
I will sell these twenty years.

And if no one heeds my cry,
the devil may choose to buy.
My heart's pure, I'll burn and loot,
if I must, I'll even shoot.

They will catch me and string me up,
with the good earth cover me up,
and death-bringing grass will start
growing from my beautiful, pure heart.

## SPRING MUD

It's raining, it's pouring
on street, park and field.
Canals gurgle, the ditch overflows,
the plaster of old buildings moulders.
Rainwater drips down horses' legs,
rainwater, blessed, pure.
There is water and mud even on rooftops,
water and mud.
The earth is all mud now, soft and warm,
and so are horses, houses, sky:
everything soft, muddy, warm.

Children are standing by windows,
they watch and listen as it pours and pours,
and their hearts, too, are
warm and soft mud.

Now the peacefulness of seeds lives
in houses, horses, people,
the peacefulness of seeds that goes deep down
where all things are akin, made
of mud, everlasting, soft and warm.

How good it feels to plunge blindly
after all my thrown-away kisses.

## APRIL 11

Tossing the heads of cut grass
and a quick peek at the sparrows
a mighty wind scooped me up once
out of an April evening's shadows.

She was looking for her children
and happened to find me on the way.
She roared her joy, I smiled, rocked
on her huge breasts lull-a-lay.

She swept me past village and field,
tumbled me good and muddy,
cackled and tugged as she dragged me
to the slushy outskirts of the city.

Playful sports loafed on the street,
getting into playful fights—
they hollered, I bawled,
till they quit and called it a night.

It must have been some big holiday,
the believers were streaming to church
where saints blessed them with sad hands
that trembled and moved with a lurch.

As bells were tolling there grew
a vast evening peace in each heart.
A murderer, finished with his man,
hat in hand, was about to depart.

In a tiny pineboard contraption
a cradled tulip and hope alive
I was promulgated in the constitution
of the year 1905.

A son to that cardloving workingman,
and for that lovely young washerwoman:
the muddy park, an ambition, a goal—
a bundle of cares wrapped in a shawl.

That poor woman's been a long time gone
but the wind won't leave her son alone.
In the forest we moan the night away
and fall asleep at the break of day.

## In Fog, In Silence

No more waiting on life for me.
I'll simply be the way I'll be.

And if there's no way, that's okay.
Even the longest day fades away.

Daylight is gone from my eyes.
Now they watch the fire rise.

If fire flames, it will burn up.
If blood must flow, there's enough.

I won't hurt those who hurt me.
I won't pity those who pity me.

You warlords can rest satisfied.
There is no hunger in my hide.

Yes, something did happen to me.
But it's not death, and not tranquility.

I've been kicked here, and kicked there,
and for once I did not swear.

I got to see the fog one time
beyond the bright lights that shine.

That was the time I had heard
that past this wild struggling world,

both above and down below
silence belongs to the poor.

Fog and silence never shine.
And now I have made them mine.

Stumbling inside me is a thing which
falls down into a blind ditch.

What a terrible, great revenge
to wait it out till all this ends.

And to know of others like me,
until someone, stunned, will see,

and seeing, will scream like a loon
in fog and silence at the moon,

up at the pestilence itself!
With a curse too horrible to tell,

cursing the keeper and the dog,
and most of all myself, in fog.

## On Evening Clouds

On evening clouds black grass sprouts, slowly
        absorbing the brightness and sprinkling
        diamond air on our sweaty faces
The world, a calm breath, floats over mountains of ice
Making them melt away
The stone we throw in the air does not fall but turning
Into a kiss it flies up on huge, warm wings,
        up, all the way up to us
The marrow in our bones glows like the polestar
In their combined light we can see the bread and water
        hiding in the palm of our hand
Tell me, what is truth, I ask the walls
Next they vanish and I see all of you under the stars
        here sitting around me.

The eyelid, silky glass, caresses when it's lowered,
        but you keep on seeing things
The aloes flower every second in our dreams
Sleeping with an unknown lover, the one whose light touch
        warns when your blanket begins to slide off.

## Attila József

*Attila József*, believe me, I love you so much, this love
    I inherited from my mother who was a blessed dear woman,
    see, she brought me into this world
We may compare life to a shoe or a dry cleaning establishment,
    but that's not why we're glad to be alive
They're ready to save the world three times a day but still can't
    even light a match — if this goes on, I've had enough
It would be nice to buy tickets for a trip into the Self;
    surely it must hide somewhere inside us
Each morning I wash my thoughts in cold water,
    so they'll be fresh and sound
Diamonds can sprout into fine, warm songs if you plant them
    under your heart
Some folks even riding a horse, a car or an airplane
    still remain pedestrian; me, I lie around in the morning
    song of larks, yet I made it past the abyss
One's true soul, like a Sunday suit, should be carefully
    saved, to remain spotless for the days of jubilation.

## WITHOUT KNOCKING

If I get to love you, please enter without knocking,
but think it over well:
my straw mattress will be yours, the dusty straw,
        the rustling sighs.

Into the pitcher fresh water I'll pour,
your shoes, before you leave, I'll wipe clean,
no one will disturb us here,
hunched over, you could mend our clothes in peace.

If the silence is great, I will talk to you,
if you are tired, take my only chair,
if it's warm here, loosen your collar, take off your tie,
if you are hungry, there's a clean sheet of paper
        as your plate if there's food,
but leave some for me—I, too, am forever hungry.

If I get to love you, enter without knocking,
but think it over well:
it would hurt if you stayed away for long.

# 1926

## WORKER

Put your tools away for a while,
set your heart free along with its steel-headed friends
there's so much I want to tell you about your forgotten
     brothers who wrap up the roots of ancient trees
where snakes huddle for warmth, to drink the gentle
     milk of stars, and begin a soothing song,
as their shadows slither out of shy children's dreams—
they pale and die off by the time the cow of heaven
     arrives bearing rich, warm gifts.

And I brought the bird, that's what you wanted,
I want to speak plainly, that's what you wanted—
all that I have touched I now place in your hands
all that they kept from you I will tell you now.

## Conjuring The Lion

I've had cigars clenched in my jaw,
had a knife stop at my wrist bone,
raging storms washed me in foam,
flies buzzed in my sleeping mouth,
auntie once napped on my bed,
poor thing, the dreams she had.
I coughed blood, which earned respect,
but I never spat blood on snow.
Once I used to taunt and jeer,
daring the dead to laugh, let's hear
if dead people live their own life!
I sipped a decent little  wine,
chewed on pig knuckles in brine,
with my left hand shook the right,
tapped my eyetooth, sold all my gods,
learned to wear these hand-me-downs,
no lame-brain can track me down:
with my spindly, overgrown heart
and love hiding behind my mirror,
I am waiting for the lion—

First and foremost, let his rich mane
buff the polish on my shoes;
second, let him caress me,
his claws tear open my throat,
and third, with his eyes closed,
let his rough tongue groom me in bed,
let him be the solitary, roaring
guard as I lie in state, dead.

## To Sit, To Stand, To Kill, To Die

To shove this chair away from here,
to squat down in front of a train,
to climb a mountain, with great care,
to empty my knapsack over the vale,
to feed a bee to my old spider,
to take an old crone, and caress her,
to sip bean soup, and eat cake,
to walk on tiptoes in the muck,
to place this hat on the railroad track,
to promenade around the lake,
to lie, all dressed up, in waters deep,
to get a suntan as waves leap,
to bloom among the sunflowers,
to let out at least one good sigh,
to shoo away a single fly,
to dust off a dusty book,
to spit at your mirror, look,
to make peace with all your foes,
to kill them all with a long knife,
to study how their blood flows,
to watch a young girl as she goes,
to sit still, and curl your toes,
to burn down the whole city,
to feed the birds, and have pity,
to hurl stale bread to the floor,
to make my good gal cry for more,
to take her little sister in my lap,
and if the world wants reasons,
to run away, not give a rap—
oh you binding and dissolving,
at this moment poem-writing,
laughing, weeping
life of my own deciding!

## THE ANT

Next to its eggs an ant has gone to sleep.
Be still, winds, do not blow them away.
Although even that would be okay.

It rests a tired head upon a grain of sand.
A tiny shadow slumbers along its side.

And now to wake it gently with a blade of grass . . .
But we'd better start for home,
the sky is overcast—

Next to its eggs lies a sleeping ant
and—oops—I felt a raindrop on my hand.

## IN THE END

I've scrubbed boilers, mowed grasses,
slept on rotting straw mattresses,
I've been sentenced, I've been mocked,
my shining light in cellars locked.
I kissed a girl who was singing
as she baked another man's bread.
I wore hand-me-downs, gave books
to workers, peasants, and they read.
Once I even loved a rich girl
but her folks snatched her away.
I ate just once every other day
but you get stomach ulcers that way.
I felt the world was an aching belly,
a churning, slimy, inflamed thing;
our minds, our loves, ulcers burning,
and war nothing but bloody vomiting.
A sourish silence filled my mouth,
I kicked my heart so it would shout.
My busy mind could never slave away
at blithe jingles, even for high pay.
I was offered coin to stall my vengeance,
the priest advised me to trust the Lord.
But when empty pockets join the fold,
you must hoe, dig, and haul stones.
Mine is a shining, victorious heart,
I must take sides and do my part,
bound by these stark memories.
But who cares about your memories?
Put that useless pen away
and start sharpening the scythe instead:
menacing, without a sound,
the time is ripening in our land.

## BELLS

Bell-making must have been
invented by someone
who could never forget
his love's blue eyes.

Bells start chiming in the trees:
someone's calling.
Dawns have many bells,
dawns
were born in young wives' hearts.

Once an angry girl threw
her small bell behind a bush.
Now she grows pale waiting
for the sound of that lost bell.
And a rich lord
hung a bell on his servant's neck.

The bell's jingle at times
flies through that servant's dreams.
If there were no bells I myself
would invent them.

## My Funeral

A smiling priest gives sunny praise
to the god of carefree grace.
Bees buzz and the mournful crowd
accompanies me down the dusty road.

A scared little girl with brown hair,
her nose to the window, wants to stare
but her father doles out a whack
with a long pipestem on her back.

And the fresh taste of dewy grass.
The morning's pink over the trees.
Grasshoppers hop, in whispering leaves
spiders wait in their webs for bees.

As my memory grows stiff and rigid
an informer slaps his forehead.
He can snoop freely around my door—
My dog won't be set on him any more.

## INTRODUCTION

My sister Lidi's brother is home,
Batu Khan's kin in Budapest,
he's lived his life on bread alone,
never had eiderdown quilts for his rest,
and for whose poems, in a huge cauldron,
Death is cooking up a feast—
hey bourgeois! hey proletarian!
Attila József is here at last!

## ENCOURAGING

In China they hanged a mandarin.
Today cocaine has killed again.
The straw is rustling, go to sleep.
Today cocaine has killed again.

Through windows of department stores
the poor see where the money goes.
The straw is rustling, go to sleep.
The poor see where the money goes.

Buy yourself sausage, buy yourself bread,
be careful and don't lose your head.
The straw is rustling, go to sleep.
Be careful and don't lose your head.

A woman who can cook and kiss:
one day you'll find even this.
The straw is rustling, go to sleep.
One day you'll find even this.

## POSTCARD FROM PARIS

The *patron* is never up in the morning,
in Paris the Berthas are called Jeanettes,
and even in barbershops you can buy
candles, spinach or suzettes.

Along the Boulevard Saint Michel
sixty nude girls sing to the sky.
The Notre Dame is cold inside;
to see the view, it's five francs a ride.

The Eiffel Tower lies down at night,
hidden by quilted fogs from the moon.
If you are a girl, the cops might kiss you.
There's no toilet seat in the men's room.

## O EUROPE

O Europe is so many borders,
on every border, murderers.
Don't let me weep for the girl
who'll give birth two years from now.

Don't let me be sad because
I was born a European.
I, a brother of wild bears,
wasting away without my freedom.

I write poems to amuse you.
The sea has risen to the cliffs,
and a table, fully laid,
floats on foam among the clouds.

## EPITAPH

He was cheerful and kind, a bit headstrong,
he spoke his mind when he was wronged.
He liked to eat, and in some ways
he resembled God.
His coat was a gift from a Jewish doc,
while from his family all he got
was: Good riddance.
He found in the Greek Orthodox
Church only priests, no peace—
he was nationwide in his decease,

but please control your grief.

# 1928

## Dappled

Here she comes, on fawn footfalls,
with a small bud in her mouth.
My well-earned and bitter pipe
drops from my magic tooth with a thud.

All those senile grasses are
suffering youthful pangs.
Who knows when they last saw
a girl with such willowy shanks?

Shazam! I'll turn to grass tonight,
weighed down by purple dew,
crisp and patient grass, so that you
may dance out your latest whims on me.

But you in your dappled dress aflail,
the minute you see me, away you turn—
so that I must grab a cool pail
to drench the grasses starting to burn.

## ÁRON JÓZSEF

Áron József was my father,
he was a soapboiler. By now,
he's mowing the fragrant grass
beyond the Great Ocean.

My mother was Borcsa Pöcze,
and cancers chewed her up.
Centipede scrubbing brushes
ate her belly, then her gut.

I loved my Lucy dearly,
but Lucy did not love me.
My furniture is shadows.
Friends? I haven't any.

All my troubles are gone now,
turned into my soul—
so I can live forever,
masterless and a fool.

## PEARL

Stars are pearls the way they shine,
it's raining pearl slivers up high,
tumbling like grapes, in clusters,
cool as raindrops, unflustered.

Although a lump of earth is pale,
clumsy and brown, it too is a pearl,
threaded by furrows onto a string,
the sad lands' beauty, an offering.

For me your hand is a star.
Alight on my head, little star.
My hand, heavy lump, a clod,
crumbles to dust on your heart.

This clumpy lump turns to dust,
a star falls, as it must.
Again the sky is a giant pearl
where our hearts are set awhirl.

## CORAL BEADS

Coral beads around your neck,
frogs' heads floating in the lake.
Lamb droppings,
lamb droppings upon the snow.

A rose in the moon's halo,
golden belt around your waist.
Hempen rope,
hempen rope around my neck.

The motion of your skirt and legs,
clappers swaying inside bells,
two poplars
bending in the river's flow.

The motion of your skirt and legs,
clappers clanging inside bells,
silent leaves
falling into flowing waves.

## GLIMMERING ROSE

In my soul's mist there she stands,
my rose bud, one single stem.
A parrot dawn flies over her,
one wing even brushes her,
but she just smiles her quiet smile
in the evening silence while
the moon pauses over her leaves
and stars settle on her thorns.

Glimmering rose, oh so sad,
around your waist, a thistle garland.
Sunshine, confined by the gloom,
locking my springtime and my dawn.
Dear lord, don't let her keel over!
Although she was born to shiver,
husky winds are prodding her,
singing snowflakes circle her.

## MEDALLIONS

### 1

I was an elephant, meek and poor,
I drank the wise waters and the cool,
stood on a hill and with my trunk
I caressed the sun, the moon,

and offered up to them a tree,
a green cricket, a snake, a flint—
now my soul is human, my heaven is gone,
I fan myself with these horrible ears.

### 3

The leech gatherer stumbles, fumbles,
the thin swineherd stares and stares,
over the lake, a heron hovers,
the fresh cowflap steams and flares,

a tired apple hangs above my head,
the worm has eaten a hole into its heart,
peeks outside, and sees the bottom,
this poem is a flower, an apple blossom.

### 4

Perhaps you are the froth on sugared milk,
or a rustling sound in the still night,
or a knife under lead-gray water,
or a button that said goodbye.

The housemaid's tears drop into the dough,
this house is burning, no kisses here for you!
If you hurry, you'll still get home—
smoldering eyes will light the way.

### 5

A pig, with knuckles of jade,
I sit on a god carved of wood.

Hey velvet mourning, appear on the milk!
When I am dead, my beard will weigh a ton.

And if I twitch my skin, the sky,
everything rolls down to my belly.
Tiny fat things will swarm all over:
O stars, you little white maggots—

6

A bright green lizard seeks out my fate,
ears of wheat rattle and spill grain,
the pond looks at me when a stone drops in,
and clouds exhaled by mourners,

dawns summoned by wars,
suns that jump and stars that vibrate
wander around my peaceful skull.
My fever is the world's red heat—

8

The lawyer squats frozen in amber,
wears black tails and stares out
with cold eyes at the loving care
lavished by light, wind, cloud—

and as I decompose, the rose blooms,
cool egrets pick me to pieces;
I shall be the warmth of autumn moons
keeping old folks free of goosepimples—

9

I share the bed with my friend,
without a wilting lily of my own,
got no machine gun, arrow or stone,
yet I'd like to kill, like everyone,

and while beans cook with sibilant pride,
you look on with cabbage-green eyes

as my feverish thick lips tremble
and barnswallows are feeding me flies—

11

Twenty-three kings promenade
with jasper crowns upon their heads,
as they nibble on cantaloupes
new moons shine in their left hands.

Twenty-three kids mill around
with beatup hats stuck on their heads,
as they gobble watermelons
new suns flame in their right hands.

# 1929

## MEDALLION

Although I didn't eat yesterday either,
the devil ate plenty in my stead—
devoured porkchops, countries, futures.
He got his belly full, and yet . . .

in place of shining moons and suns,
it's my own wild excrements that shine
as medallions of swinish death!
They're singing and having a good time . . .

## The Rain Falls

I stand watching the puddle grow
into a mire—doing its job.
Tail between legs, a dog
creeps up to sniff my foot.
The heavens are swollen,
their business is salvation.
The bishop's fat lands
shimmer and get fatter.
I try to whistle, and blow steam,
so I steam beautifully
and look important, calm, collected
like a weed. And I sink into reverie.

I used to whistle in my breezier days . . .
Now the rain falls, mud and weeds rise.
On the ground only a cool carrot,
a harmless paintbrush, and I
listen and give thought.

The sluggish, nationwide rain
laments my thinning hair.

I am a growler, so I growl,
and a stroller, so I stroll:
you don't need oars for the highway.

My shoes mumble and grumble,
this is too much even for boots.

A pumpkin fidgets, a haystack mopes,
this rain falls on barefoot people,
falls on workers out of work,
falls on the trembling tower,
on estates and on the soft soil,
on cave-dwelling migrant workers,
on cushioned suburban homes,
the rain falls, just doing its job.

Sluggish, nationwide rain,
heavy with complaints.

## TISZAZUG

Pine needles stitch lambskin
shadows to the trees.
Like a sheepdog, the moment spins,
claws clicking on ice.

The mesmerized folk hem and haw.
Their little houses brood
and lower the greasy hood
of thatch over their windows.

A wretched hen clucks, lost
under the eaves, an
old woman's ghost,
returned to complain.

Indoors, other spotted beasts—
blue, battered old people squat
grunting aloud from time to time
so they won't sink into thought.

For there is much to think about
when you are too old for the hoe.
Pipesmoke is a fine, soft care,
cotton yarn for cracked fingers to hold.

What good are old folks? They drop
the spoon, drool, have to be fed.
Trying to feed the pigs
they stumble and spill the slops.

The farm is soft, the pigsty warm.
Twilight hangs there from a star.
Heaven is hard. A titmouse hobbles
on a twig, and twitters out a cry.

## WOODCUTTER

I chop the wood into a cool pile,
screeching knots and gnarls all shine,
hoarfrost falls on my flying hair,
and down my neck to tickle there—
    my minutes glide by on velvet.

Winter's axe glitters on high,
flashing on earth, sky, forehead, eye.
Dawn lashes out, splinters of light fly,
another cutter grumbles nearby,
    "I cut the trunk and get the twigs."

Oh, strike at the roots instead of wailing,
don't wince at splinters, stop quailing!
If you aim your blows at fate
the lordly wasteland will hate
    you, but your broad axe will smile.

# 1930

## SUMMER

Golden plain, marigold,
streamlined, weightless fields.
A small breeze shakes silver cheer
from a birch. The sky sways.

Here comes a bee, comes to sniff me,
bumbling, it lands on a wild rose.
The angry rose kowtows—
this crimson summer's still young.

More and more soft stirrings.
Blood-red berries on the sand.
Ears of wheat nodding and rustling.
A storm is perched above the land.

My summer's end is here so fast!
The wind rides wheeling tumbleweed—
and my comrades, as the heavens crash,
I see the flash of the first scythe blade.

## GRIEF

I fled like the deer,
tender grief in my eyes.
Tree-gnawing wolves
were chasing in my heart.

I lost my antlers way back,
they swing on a branch, broken.
Although I was a deer, alack,
now I'll be a wolf, heartbroken.

I'll make a neat little wolf.
At a magic stroke, I'll stop—
my howling fellows foaming at the mouth—
and try to smile, if I still know how.

Straining my ears for a doe's cry
I will close my eyes in sleep.
Dark mulberry leaves will fall
and cover my shoulders in a heap.

## MOTHER

She held the mug with both hands
one Sunday, and with a quiet smile
she sat a little while
in the growing dusk.

In a small saucepan she brought home her
dinner from the rich folks where she worked.
Going to bed, I kept thinking
that some folks eat a whole potful.

My mother was a small woman,
she died early, like most washerwomen:
their legs tremble from lugging the hamper,
their heads ache from ironing.

For mountains, they have those piles of laundry.
Their cloudscapes are made of steam.
And for a change of climate,
there's the attic stairs to climb.

I see her pausing with the iron.
Her frail body, grown thinner and thinner,
was at last broken by Capital.
Think about this, my fellow have-nots.

She was so stooped from all that laundry
I did not realize she was still a young woman.
In her dreams she wore a clean apron,
and the mailman would say hello to her.

## WASTELAND

Water smokes, withered sedge
droops at the plain's edge.
The heights are clad in feathery puffs.
A thick silence huffs
        in the fields.

Fat dusk spreads greasily around
the flat, sparse lowland without a sound.
Only a rowboat may be heard
clucking to itself on a freezing pond
        in monotone.

In labor, the forest's icy branches clatter
giving birth to this season that rattles.
This is where frost snaps and finds moss
and ties up its bony horse,
        let him rest.

In the vineyards, scattered plum trees.
Vinestocks wear soggy straw against the freeze.
Row upon row of skinny stakes
such as old peasants would take
        for a walk.

And the farmhouse, around which this landscape
revolves. Winter's claws scrape,
playfully, some more plaster
from its walls that fester,
        crumbling.

The pigsty's gate is wide open, creaking.
It hangs loose, the wind's plaything.
Perhaps a lost pig will wander inside
or a whole cornfield come running here to hide,
        full of corn!

Small peasants in a small room.
One of them smokes, but only dry leaves.
No prayer is going to help these.
They just sit in the gloom,
        full of thought.

The freezing vineyard is the landlord's.
His are the forest's trees, in hordes.
The pond is his, and the ice,
and every fat fish that lies
        in the mud.

# FROST

Autumn was wild and brooding.
Pensive snow would like to fall now.
But the season is impatient, drumming
on hard frost's clear window.

Now is the season of bankers and generals,
this present time,
this hammer-hardened cold,
this flashing, this knife time.

Steel clanks in the armored sky.
This frost pierces the lung, stabs
the naked breast under the rags—
O screeching grinding-wheel time!

Behind it, so many silent, cold
tin cans and bread loaves,
piles of frozen goods!
O season of shop windows.

And people shout, "Pass
that stone! Gimme that lead pipe!
Kill! Stomp! Smash!"
O what a time, what a time—

## NIGHT IN THE SLUMS

Daylight slowly draws
its net up from our yard
and like a hole in the bottom of a pool
our kitchen is filled by the dark.

Silence. A sluggish scrubbing brush
almost manages to crawl.
Above, a sliver of plaster
ponders whether it should fall.

And night, wrapped up in oily rags,
stoops and sighs in the sky,
sits down by the city's outskirts,
staggers across a square in fits and starts,
uncovers a bit of moon for a light.

The factories
stand like ruins,
but inside
a thicker darkness is laid down,
the foundation of silence.

Through windows of textile plants
moonlight descends
in sheaves.
The moon's soft light is the yarn
woven by ribbed looms.
Until dawn, when work begins again,
machines sullenly weave
factory girls' cascading dreams.

Nearby, graveyard arcades:
steel mills, cement works, powerplants.
So many echoing family crypts.
These factories guard the secret
of a mournful resurrection.
A cat claws the planks of a fence
and the superstitious watchman sees
a will-o'the wisp, quick flashing lights—
as beetle-backed dynamos
shine cold and bright.

A trainwhistle.

Dampness rummages in the gloom
among leaves of a fallen tree
and weighs down
the street's dust.
ÆPGØ
In the alley, a policeman and a mumbling worker.
An occasional comrade carrying handbills
scurries by catlike,
avoiding streetlamps, listening
for noises from behind,
sniffing around like a dog.

The door to a bar vomits foul light,
its window spews out a puddle;
a drowning lamp swings inside,
and while the bartender snores wheezing,
a lone day laborer keeps the wake.
He grits his teeth at the wall.
His grief wells up step by step,
he weeps and salutes the revolution.

Like molten ore that's cooled,
crashing waters solidify.
The wind, stray dog, roams loose
large tongue hanging out,
reaching the water, lapping it up.
Straw mattresses, like rafts,
silently drift on night's tide.

The warehouse is a grounded ark,
the foundry an iron barge.
The iron caster dreams a red infant
into metal dies.

All is dank, all is so heavy.
Poverty's domains are mapped out
by mildew on the wall.
Out on the barren fields, rags
on the ragged grass, and a scrap
of paper. How it wants to move!
It stirs, but has no strength to fly.

O night
your damp and clinging wind is nothing
but dirty bedsheets fluttering.
O night
you hang from the sky like threadbare linen
on a clothesline, like sorrow dangling in our lives!
O night of the poor, be my fuel,
smolder here in my heart,
smelt from me the iron,
the unbreakable anvil,
the clanging, flashing hammer,
and the sharp blade of victory,
o night.

The night is heavy, this somber night.
Brothers, I am going to sleep.
May our souls be free of torment,
and our bodies free of vermin's bite.

# Rain

Scythes in the sky are flashing,
swaths of rain come tumbling down,
rustling stalks of rain fall crashing
in broad thick sheaves onto the ground.
Like grains of wheat the raindrops
crackle and dance on rooftops.

Scythes flashing? No, bayonets.
Shopwindows rattle in the rat-tat
of bullets, a tattoo of running feet
shoots up a flame. Their teeth clenched,
the masses of the earth arise in revolt.
Dark fluid pours in rivulets.

Or is it only the machine's roar
as it weaves the supple, soft fabric?
To blanket the tortured land the way
humming spindles lull the tired brain?
Old mother autumn brought us a round mirror:
what do you see in it, proletarians?

## In The Fields

A bumblebee roams past a thicket of trees,
a woodpecker pecks, a lizard shines.
Cattle low.  A curly, ruffling breeze
marks this meditative, humming time.

Yellow land, crushed against the breast of the sky,
its millet field a heavy, starched apron—what
does it contain? A running brook, a squat
farmhouse and its small progeny, the pigsty.

The dusty water refuses to shine.
A road winds its scaly back among rustling pine.
On it the old men of this age
escape in flocks from their crumbling village.

They hope to find their bread under a foreign yoke.
Their gait is slow, this brown and bony folk.
Their small bundles huddle on wheelbarrows.
Above, soft knapsacks of clouds loosen their billows.

Hissing dust and mud bespatter them.
Where will they find their work and bread?
A hesitant mosquito wails, and the dry-
eyed fields stare straight ahead.

## THE SEVENTH

If you set foot on this earth,
you must go through seven births.
Once, in a house that's burning,
once, among ice floes churning,
once, amidst madmen raving,
once, in a field of wheat swaying,
once, in a cloister, bells ringing,
once, in a pigsty a-squealing.
Six babes crying, not enough, son.
Let yourself be the seventh one!

If foes confront you, that is when
your enemies must see seven men.
One, who's off on a holiday,
one, who goes to work on Monday,
one, who teaches unpaid on a whim,
one, who has learned to sink or swim,
one, who will seed a whole forest,
one, whom wild forefathers protect.
But all their tricks are not enough, son.
Let yourself be the seventh one!

If you want to find a lover,
let seven men go look for her.
One, whose words contain his heart,
one, who can pay his part,
one, pretending to be a dreamer,
one, who will be a skirt-peeler,
one, who knows the snaps and hooks,
one, who can put down his foot—
buzz like flies around her, son.
And you yourself be the seventh one.

Be a poet if you can afford it,
but seven men make up one poet.
One, a marble-village builder,
one, who was born a sleeper,
one, an adept sky-charter,
one, whom words befriend and favor,
one, who is his own soul-maker,

and one who dissects a rat's liver.
Two are brave and four are wise, son—
let yourself be the seventh one.

And if all went as was written,
you will be buried as seven men.
One, nursed on a soft milky breast,
one, who likes tough titties best,
one, who flips empty plates in the bin,
one, who helps the poor to win,
one, who labors, falling apart,
one, who stares at the Moon all night.
The world will be your tombstone, son:
if you yourself are the seventh one.

## TREES

Among the rainsoaked, juicy furrows
      of ploughed land
mournful trees await in rows
      the quick flatchested fog.

Their yellow leaves droop down,
      their trunks shine, wet.
All cried out, they stand alone
      in the quick sunset.

They stand there tall, unpruned, raw
      timber for cudgels.
In place of bright fruit, a squat crow
      meditates and huddles.

The terrified roots desperately cling
      to the eroding ground.
The sap still runs, the trees exhale
      with a rustling sound.

These murmuring trees are dreaming of buds.
      The sky is vast, open and clear—
The cold blue steel of ethics will flash
      when morning is here.

## THE NET

My hair falls out, I have no bread,
    my pen is worn,
my uncle the fisherman is dead.
    But I'm not alone.

I drag the network of my nerves,
    my fishing net,
in heavy waters to catch light dreams
    and daily bread.

It must be torn, I think,
    my poor net.
So I hang it up to mend it,
    and see that

spread out, my frozen net
    is the bright firmament—
its icy knots with stars
    resplendent.

## A Child Is Crying

In a dark corner of the room
cries a helpless, crouching child.
He cries like sand under a boot.
He thrashes, like a heavy tide.

He is tearful as a northern vale.
He is tearful as a tear-filled eye.
Tearful, as the soil under a stone.
Tearful, as the windowpane.

He cries, as quicklime cries in water.
Cries, like water boiling in a pot.
Cries, like dead wood in the fire.
Cries, like factory assembly lines.

Cries, like the wind
carrying the living warmth
of people, plants, animals
to polar cliffs, blowing icy dust.

Screams, like New Year's pig, afraid.
Screams, like the knife being honed.
Screams, like rye cut by the blade.
Meat screams like this when it is baked.

. . . Like an office drudge who quietly goes home,
folds up his clothes and lays them down,
lies on his bed dreaming and growls,
slips away with quick, small footfalls

and trots out to the plain in green moonglow,
in the frozen night he tastes the snow,
yelps and scrapes, would lick the sky's salt—
howling alone in the wasteland . . .

Whimpers, like corn being husked.
Whimpers, like straw by a sleeper crushed.

Whimpers, like an idiot oppressed by time.
Whimpers, like a dog whipped into line.

In a dark corner of the room
cries a helpless, crouching child.
Like a motor, he idles high,
then slows down, like a heavy tide.

## WINTER NIGHT

Be disciplined!

Summer's flame
has blown out.
Above the broad charred lumps it covers
a fine light ash stirs and hovers.
A place of silence,
this air,
this fine crystal atmosphere
scraped only by a sharp twig or two.
A lovely people-lessness.  Only a shred
of tinselly scrap—some ribbon or rag—
clings fiercely to a bush,
for all the smiles and hugs snagged
in this thornful world.

In the distance, knobby old hills stand
ponderous, like tired hands,
shifting at times to guard
the sunset's flame,
the steaming farmhouse,
the vale's round silence, the breathing moss.

A farm worker heads home, weighed down,
each heavy limb earthbound.
The cracked hoe on his shoulder rambles
along, shaft and blade a bloody shambles.
As if returning home, leaving life itself,
his body and tools both prove
heavier with each move.

Night flies up scattering stars,
like smoke from a chimney belching sparks.

This blue and iron night comes floating
on the stately waves of bells tolling.
Feels like my heart's stopped, forever still,
and what throbs, with bated breath,
is perhaps the land itself, not death.
As if the winter night, winter sky, winter ore

created a bell,
its clapper the hammered earth, the swaying core—
and my heart sounding its knell.

Clangor's echo floats, heard by the mind.
Winter struck the anvil: iron to bind
the heavenly vault's dangling gate,
that poured all that fruit, light, wheat, hay
while summer held sway.

Like thought itself, the winter night
is bright.

This muteness, this silvery dark
makes the moon the world's padlock.

The raven flies, silence grows cool
across cold space. Bone, can you hear the silence?
Molecule clinks against molecule.

In what showcase shine lights
such as this winter night's?

Frost sticks daggers in twiggy hands
and the wasteland's
black sigh soughs—
drifting in fog, a flock of crows.

In this winter night a freight
train—itself a small winter night—
streaks out onto the plain.
Its smoke ready to extinguish,
in an armspan infinity,
the stars that revolve and languish.

On the frozen tops of boxcars
scurrying like a mouse, light flies,
the light of this winter night.

Above cities, up high
winter still steams up the sky.
But on the flashing track

blue frost brings racing back
the light of this jaundiced night.

In city workshops is where it's made,
mass-produced pain's cold steel blade,
by the light of this frigid night.

On the outskirts of town,
in streetlight like wet straw flung down,
off to the side
on the corner, a shivering coatful of woes:
a man, hunkered down like a pile of dirt,
but winter still steps on his toes  . . .

Where a rusty-leafed tree
leans out of the dark,
like an owner
his property,
I measure the winter night.

# WITHOUT HOPE

## Slowly, Meditatively

In the end you reach the sand
on a sad, marshy plain
where in a reverie you look around
and nod, never to hope again.

I try to see things that way:
straight and sans souci,
while silvery axe strokes play
with the leaves of the ash tree.

My heart is perched on a branch of nothing,
its tiny form trembles without a sound,
and the stars gently gather
to stare at it from all around.


## In an Iron-colored Sky

A cold and shiny dynamo revolves
in an iron-colored sky.
O noiseless constellations!
From my teeth, word-sparks fly—

Inside me the past is falling
like a silent stone through space.
This mute blue time flutters away.
The swordblade flashing is my hair—

My mustache, fat caterpillar, droops
over my mouth, whose taste is gone.
My heart aches, words grow cold.
But who is there to hear me out—

## YELLOW GRASSES

Yellow grasses on the sand,
the wind is a gaunt old woman,
the puddle a nervous beast,
the sea is calm and tells a tale.

I hum my inventory's gentle tune.
A pawned overcoat is my home,
the sunset crumbling on the dune,
I haven't the heart to go on.

They shine, time's teeming
coral reef, the dead world,
birch tree, woman, tenement—
across the sky's blue whirl.

## On The City's Edge

On the city's edge where I live,
when sunset comes caving in,
like so many tiny bats
soot floats down on soft wings
settling into a crust of guano,
a hard and thick skin.

That is how this present age squats
on our souls. And like a dense ragged
downpour washing, rub-a-dub,
a jagged tin roof's sides—
grief attempts in vain to scrub
the grime encrusted on our hearts.

It might take a bloodbath, the way we're made.
We are another type, a new breed.
We speak a new language, even our hair
hugs our heads in a different style.
We were created, not by god, or reason
but by oil, coal and iron,

the actual materials we're made of,
splashed hot and furious
into the moulds of this monstrous
misshapen form of society
so that we may stand up for all humanity
upon this eternal soil.

After the priest, soldier and burgher
now it is our turn at last
to be upholder of the laws;
and so the sense of all human works
resonates in us
like so many resounding violas.

We are indestructible, although
since the solar system began to jell,
in history's long procession
in untold numbers we fell,
killed by weapons and starvation,
disease and hatred's hell.

No destined winner has ever
been humiliated as much as we
were humiliated here
under the stars:
so we cast down our eyes. And found
the secret buried underground.

Behold the dearest props of this age,
see the machines go on a rampage!
Fragile villages snap and crumble
as a puddle's skin of ice—
cities fall when machines rumble
and pound the skies.

Who would control them? Is it the landlord
the shepherd's fierce dog obeys?
The machine's childhood, and ours, was the same.
We grew up together, we know its ways.
For us, the beast will act tame.
It will listen to those who know its name.

We know that before long
all of you will be on your knees
worshipping machines,
things you merely own.
But machines have their own way,
the one who feeds them is the one they obey . . .

So here we are, distrustful, gathered
together, the children of matter.
Lift up our hearts! For they belong
to the benefactor.
But to be strong enough for that
one must be made of our matter.

Lift up these hearts, high above factories!
Such a sooty great heart
is known only to those who saw the sun
set in factory smoke and drown,
who heard the throbbing mineshafts,
in the pit, deep underground.

Arise! . . . Around this parceled-out land
the plank fence cries, and stands
staggering as in a raging storm,
to crash when our breath's expelled.
Let's blow it away! Lift up your heart,
let it smoke overhead!

When our finest potential's realized—
order shining bright—
then the mind can at last grasp
both the endless, and the finite:
the forces of production outside,
and the instincts, here, inside  . . .

On the city's edge my song is shrill.
The poet, your next of kin,
can only look on, and watch
the fat and soft soot fall and begin
settling into a crust of guano,
a hard and thick skin.

The poet's mouth stutters the word,
but he (as engineer
of magic in this world)
can see a fully conscious future
and plans, inside, what you will build—
the design of harmony he'd glimpsed.

# ELEGY

Like a dense downdrift of smoke
between sad land and leaden sky
my soul swings low,
close to the ground.
It stirs, but cannot fly.

O heavy soul, supple imagination!
Follow reality's ponderous tread,
take a look at yourself
here, where you originated.
Here, under a sky at other times so pale,
near a solitary wall, gaunt and bare,
poverty's sullen silence,
menacing, pleading,
dissolves the grief
hardened on the brooding heart
and stirs it
into those of millions.

The whole man-made world
is prepared here, where all is in ruins.
In the abandoned factory yard
a hardy dandelion opens a parasol.
The days go down
the faded steps of broken little windows
into damp shadows.
Answer now:
are you from here?
Are you from here, never free
of the grim desire to be
like every other miserable creature
on whom this vast age stamped itself,
deforming each face, every feature?

Here you can rest, where a battered fence
with its shrill posted cries
upholds and tries
to guard a greedy moral order.
Do you recognize yourself? Waiting here
for that fine, well-planned, secure future

are souls with the emptiness of vacant lots
lying around in a mournful daze
dreaming of tall buildings that weave
the busy hum of life. The tortured grass
is watched by dull, fixed eyes:
broken glass set in mud that dries.

From time to time a thimbleful of sand
rolls from a mound. And at times
a green or blue or black fly
buzzes by,
drawn here by human waste and rags
from richer regions.
Sucked dry by Capital and Interest,
blessèd mother earth sets
the table even here: in a rusty pot,
yellow grass blooms bright.

Can you tell
what barren joy, what relentless swell
of consciousness pushed-pulled you here,
what rich suffering
tossed you on this shore?
This is how the child, beaten by a stranger,
comes running home to his mother.
Only here
can you truly smile or cry.
Only here, no matter how you try,
can you bear yourself, my soul!
This is your home.

# ODE

### 1

I sit on a glittering rock.
Young summer's light breeze
floats like the warmth
of a dinner for two.
I am getting my heart used to silence.
It is not very hard to do—
the past comes swarming back
when the head bends down
and the hands hang low.

I look upon the mountain's mane—
each leaf reflects
the light of your face.
The road is empty, empty—
but I can still see
your skirt flutter in the wind.
And under fragile branches
your hair tumbles forward,
your breasts softly sway,
and, as the brook trickles away,
laughter springs again
on the round white pebbles
that are your teeth.

### 2

O how I love you
who could bring to words
both solitude, that furtive plotter
in the deepest hollows of the heart,
and a whole universe.
Who, like a waterfall from its own thunder,
part from me and run quietly on,
while I, among the summits of my life,
in the nearness of the far,
resound and scream,
thrashing against earth and sky,
my love for you, sweet stepmother!

3

I love you like a child his mother,
like silent caves their depths,
love you as rooms love light,
the soul loves flames, and the body, rest.
I love you as the living
love life until they die.

I save each of your smiles, gestures, words,
the way dropped objects are saved by the earth.
The way acid marks metal with its bite
I have etched you into the instincts of my mind:
your beautiful, dear form
becomes and fills all meaning.

Minutes march by with a clatter
but you reside in the silence of my ears.
Stars flare up and shatter
but you stand still in my eyes.
Your taste, like silence in a cavern,
lingers cool on my tongue,
and your delicately veined hand,
holding a glass of water,
reappears again and again.

4

O what is this stuff I am made of
that your glance can rend and shape?
What soul, what light,
what wondrous magic might
lets me roam in the fog of nothingness
through the rolling hills of your lush body?

And like the word entering the opened mind,
into your mysteries I descend . . .

Your arteries and veins are rosebushes
that ceaselessly quiver.
They circulate the endless stream
so that upon your face love may bloom,

and blessed fruit grow in your womb.
Your belly's sensitive soil
is embroidered through and through
by a multitude of tiny filaments
weaving their fine thread into knots
raveled and unraveled so that your fluid
cells may gather into flocks
and your leafy lungs' thickets
may whisper their own praise!

Eternal matter moves serenely
down your bowels' dump
and even slag gains a richer life
through your kidneys' hot pump.

In you, undulating hills arise,
constellations tremble,
lakes quiver, factories produce,
a myriad living creatures,
seaweed,
insects whir,
cruelty and goodwill stir,
suns shine, northern lights glimmer—
in your substance resides
eternity, the unconscious.

5

Like clotted drops of blood,
these words flutter
at your feet.
Existence stutters,
only the laws speak clearly.
My hard-working organs
that give me new birth each day
are getting ready to grow silent.

Yet until then, they all cry out
to you, the only one
chosen from the multitude
of two thousand million,

o you soft cradle, firm grave,
living bed, take me in! . . .

(How high is the dawn sky!
In its ores, whole armies glitter.
This brilliance hurts my eyes.
I am lost, I surrender.
Overhead I can hear
my heartbeat flutter.)

6

*(Envoi)*

(The train takes me in your wake,
I may even reach you today.
Perhaps my burning face will cool,
perhaps you will quietly say,

"Take a bath in the warm water.
Here's a towel, get yourself dry.
Dinner's cooking, to soothe your hunger.
This is your bed, where I lie.")

## FREIGHT TRAINS

Freight trains switching,
their dreamy clanging
claps light handcuffs
on the mute landscape.

The moon flies, as easy
as a prisoner set free.

Crushed stones
lie on their own shadows,
sparkle
for themselves,
they are in place,
as never before.

From what vast dark
was this heavy night chipped?
It falls on us
like a chunk of iron on a speck of dust.

Desire, born of the sun,
when the bed is embraced by shadow,
could you stay awake
all through
that night?

## Summer Afternoon

Shears chatter. Sister,
  trimming the lawn,
stops. Even from behind
  you can see her yawn.

The radio squirms. Wings
  buzz on the windowpane,
breezes dance and swing
  on the soft lawn.

Time plays at being nothing,
  a warm puddle, it stops.
You can see that it still flies:
  a flower petal drops.

I can't even tell any more:
  am I asleep or writing or both?
My wife sets the table
  with a fine white cloth.

Even the sky is flooded here
  with a white linen glare.
Wild strawberries shine
  in a glass bowl on a chair.

I am happy. My love
  sews by my side.
We listen to an old freight
  train whistle out of sight.

## Consciousness

I

Dawn unbinds the sky from the earth
and at its clear soft word
beetles and children
spin forth into the world:
there is no haze in the air,
this bright clarity floats everywhere.
Overnight, they have covered the trees:
like so many small butterflies, the leaves.

II

I saw paintings daubed with red,
yellow and blue in my dreams,
and I felt it was all in order,
not a speck of dust out of place.
Now my dreams seem pale shadows haunting
my limbs; the iron world order returns.
During the day a moon rises within
and inside me at night the sun burns.

III

I am thin, at times I eat only bread.
Among souls that idly chatter and temporize
I search—free and free of charge—
for greater certainty than the fall of dice.
Stuffing myself with roast beef would be nice,
or cuddling a small child to my heart—
but even the trickiest cat can't catch at once
the mouse outside and the one in the house.

IV

Just like a pile of split wood
the world lies in a heap;
so does each thing push, uphold, keep
every other thing in place,
so that everything is determined.

Only what is not can become a tree,
only what's yet to come can be a flower.
The things that exist fall into pieces.

V

As a child at the freight station I lay
in wait, flattened against a tree
like a piece of silence. Gray
weeds touched my mouth, raw, strangely sweet.
Dead still, I watched the guard's feet,
his passing shadow on the boxcars
stubbornly kept falling over my prize,
those scattered lumps of coal, dewy and bright.

VI

The anguish is deep inside me, here,
while its explanation lies out there.
My wound is the whole world—it burns;
I feel the fever, my soul, as it churns.
You are enslaved by your rebellious heart,
and will be free only when you stop
building yourself the kind of apartment
where a landlord moves in to collect rent.

VII

I looked up in the night
at the cogwheels of the stars:
from sparkling threads of chance
the loom of the past wove laws.
Then, in my steaming dream
I looked at the sky again:
somehow the fabric of the law
always had a missing stitch, a flaw.

VIII

Silence listened, the clock struck one.
Why not visit your childhood—
even among cinderblock walls one could

imagine some bit of freedom,
I thought. But when I stood up,
the constellations, the Big Bear
like prison bars, shone up there
above my silent cell.

IX

I have heard iron crying,
I have heard rain laughing.
I have seen the past split apart
and realize only notions can be forgot;
that all I can do is keep loving
while bent double under my burdens.
Why should I forge a swordblade
out of you, golden consciousness!

X

An adult is someone bereft
of father and mother inside his heart,
who knows that life is a free gift,
something extra thrown in on death's part,
and, like a found object, can be returned
any time—therefore, it's to be treasured.
He is nobody's god or priest
—his own self's least.

XI

Once I saw happiness, contentment:
four hundred pounds of rotund pink fat.
Over the harsh grass of the farmyard
its curly smile swayed and tottered.
It plopped down in a puddle, warm and nice,
looked at me, blinked, grunted twice—
I still see the hesitant way
light fumbled in its bristles as it lay.

XII

I live by the railroad tracks,
watching all the trains go by.

The shining windows fly
in the swaying downy darkness.
This is how in eternal night
the lit-up days speed by
and I stand in the light of each compartment,
leaning on my elbow, silent.

## VILLAGE

The small village, this lazy evening,
    with its heap of red tiles
is like a plate of languidly steaming
    stew: potatoes *paprikás*.

Here and there a wisp of smoke—or hope?
    wavers before it escapes,
pausing at chimney's tip, to grope,
    greeting the landscape.

Dusk fondles a slim young locust tree.
    Its small round breast shivers
and sets a diminutive sigh free,
    an airy butterfly that quivers.

And I am wrapped in the silent boughs
    of a mellow reverie
so that a dog's distant barking falls
    on mute velvet around me.

Women light the lamps. Flames
    twitch and strain, and would fly
like so many souls in chains
    up, up, into the sky.

They all flicker out  .  .  .  Only one light
    illumines the field,
the motherly moon, so bright
    that a sumac bough offers its shield.

Waves of eternal happiness caress
    a hoarse, cracked old brick.
I see emerald Buddhas in the dewy grass
    where toads sit, still and quick.

Having drawn their swords, now wild oats
    bend their heads, repentant.
And in moonlight the tumbledown barn floats
    power and glory exultant.

. . . Inside, it's silent. As if some sound
        had only just flown off,
save for its silence, gone,
        unheard, merely thought of.

As knowledge dawns, it gathers here
        the things that do not fade,
the only possible words in the air:
        like plough and spade.

Words that the farmer says, talking
        to the earth, sun, and rain.
Words used by the poet, trusting
        in future times' care.

Words that smile at the suckling babe
        and pat the horse's back.
Words; words with syllables that make
        clear sense, and won't crack . . .

. . . I listen to the village dreaming.
        Our troubled visions pass;
they prod and flutter the sleeping
        shadowy blades of grass.

Skies and fields, whips, knives, and boots,
        all are sound asleep,
the empty spaces between each bough,
        each and every leaf.

And asleep each raw, slow-spoken
        weathered peasant.
Like grief on their hearts, I sit on
        a small hill, vigilant.

## TERROR

The one-room apartment is dark.
In the alcove a baby is waking
wrapped in rags, moaning
with pursed lips, jerky, twitching,

it stirs, shivers like a puddle
brushed by cold autumn winds.
A small girl, deep in thought
sits in another corner of the room.

Two of them share the sleeping alcove,
both lives fueled by desire and hate.
She and her Teddy bear, much worn,
like the historical print on the wall.

The girl is seven. She'd love to run off.
Indoors you can't even jump around.
Mom made her promise she would take care
of this little beast, the infant.

Oh she'd run and run! But this reverie
almost puts her to sleep.
She feels enough energy
to tear the whole city down.

But the swollen eyelids open, and at once
the tiny baby boy begins to bawl.
The girl looks on in silence,
and goes to warm milk in a bowl.

She stares ahead serenely at peace
watching the baby turn blue in the face.
In her dull hair the ribbon dangling
resembles a dead butterfly's wing.

Then she shoves the nippled bottle
into the gaping, howling maw.
The baby coughs and chokes, throttled,
and cries like a broken stick now.

His tiny body quakes like the sea.
The nipple drips, a leaky faucet.
And when the girl takes it away
he howls, gulps, snaps after it.

When all he can do is gape and strain,
the girl shoves the bottle back in;
when he calms down, sucking,
the bottle is snatched away again.

The baby is torn between pleasure
and rage; shaken, he cries on the rack.
His lips are covered with curds
that his small gullet keeps sending back.

Now he's as red as a newborn.
The veins on his head
swell, writhing like worms,
his big toe rigidly extends.

He bleats, quacks, terrified,
gums snap at the empty dark.
Only parents of newly born gods
could feel such utter terror.

He's damp with dread. If she gives,
why does she take away?
The girl is stony as a killer.
Outside, blind musicians play.

She plays this game for hours on end
without a word or smile.
When the woman from next door knocks,
she starts and answers, all sweet guile,

through the door, "The poor darling
is probably teething."
And back to the alcove, to linger
there playing with her thin fingers.

For weeks now, the mother, home at night,
takes her son in her lap, but

though he clutches her with all his might
the sweet milk he will not take.

Seeing the bottle, he starts to cry,
wants only to cuddle in her warmth,
and tremble there with closed eyes
like a broken old man.

The mother can't imagine what's wrong.
(She at last takes off her scarf.)
The daughter glibly prattles on:
"I fed him on time.

Mama, will you let me cook tonight?"
She wheedles, by now in a good mood.
But the mother is wasted, she knows
she must rest, get to bed . . .

At night, there are no stars.
The seasons wail past, and skies.
In her dream, the mother sobs and starts,
thinking it's her baby that cries.

Only a mute whimper's frozen on his face.
When she gets up to take a peep,
she imagines her child smiling, at peace . . .
Her mind at ease, she goes back to sleep.

Up at dawn, hurrying off to work,
she prepares a small snack, and must be off.
The girl is up, too, and getting dressed
she makes solemn vows, promises.

But her solitude is too great to take.
She's propelled outside by anguish and pain.
Again the baby cries out, awake—
and everything starts all over again.

## On The Pavement

On the pavement a small puddle was blinking
as shadows began to occupy the streets.
In their restless dreams sparrows were chirping
but then silently hung on to their twigs.
The sleeping ones will always cling
harder than the awake, ready to take flight.
People, streetcars, taxis were bustling
just like the instincts and the mind.

I kissed a girl on her mouth in a doorway,
then I mixed in among the crowd again,
only to separate from it once more, so that
this poem could crystallize from life's pain.
At last I see, after long meditation,
my animal sorrow is understandable
human grief that finds its scintillation
even in advertising displays.

## Lullaby

Now the sky shuts its blue eyes,
in our house, out go the lights,
a quilt covers the hillside—
goodnight little one, sleep tight.

The ladybug and the dragonfly
have gone to sleep, they don't cry,
the bees' buzz goes to sleep for the night—
goodnight little one, sleep tight.

The streetcar sleeps out on the street,
and while the rumbling goes beddy-bye,
the dreaming bell clangs once, ever so light—
goodnight little one, sleep tight.

Your clothes are asleep on the chair,
your jacket is dozing, the tear
on it won't rip any more tonight—
goodnight little one, sleep tight.

Your ball is asleep, and your flute,
outdoors the fields, and the woods,
and the fat candy bar at your bedside—
goodnight little one, sleep tight.

And outer space, like a clear
marble, will be yours, you'll be
a giant when you close your eyes—
goodnight little one, sleep tight.

You'll be a fireman, you'll drive a jeep!
You'll tame wild beasts in the night!
Look, even your mom is going to sleep—
goodnight little one, sleep tight.

## I Open A Door

I open a door. The stale smell
of cooking sluggishly withdraws
and the stove on its iron claws
snarls across the kitchen. The room

is empty, abandoned. Sixteen years
have passed and I still cannot forget.
The canvas chair is there, I sit down
and want to whimper, but can't.

I know mother's been buried.
But she's not here, this troubles me,
this I cannot grasp. I could be a grownup.
(The kitchen sink shines spotlessly clean.)

It doesn't hurt, but I didn't touch her,
was not allowed to see my dead mother,
I didn't cry. And I cannot fathom
this is how it'll be from now on.

## MODERN SONNET

One lives on, though the larder's cleaned out
and the breadbox is empty of bread.
You are kept alive by fear of death.
(In this harsh moment I confront myself.)

Though I can live with it, I now regret
there's no God to watch over my sighs
and to pluck out those eyes
that look on while I must go without bread.

I used to be so proud in my misery!
But only the mule is proud, now I see,
when the whip cracks over his back, loud,

and the new recruit on his first honor guard,
and the child who wins the school spelling bee,
given apple pie at home as a reward.

## HUMANS

In our human family goodness is a stranger.
Selfishness is the landlord in this place.
For ages the rich have unthinkingly known this;
now it is beginning to dawn on the poor.

All weavings come unraveled in the end.
We who proudly claim to be the righteous
hide the criminal in our unconscious.
The tune is different, but the words remain.

But still, we sing out loud, all is cool,
and steel ourselves with pills and alcohol
on empty stomachs, crooning the blues.

To be righteous, be skilled at bad news.
Of tiny, biting reasons we are as full
as a whispering willow rife with mosquitoes.

## BE A FOOL

Be a fool! Don't worry, freedom in this age
is only for fools. We are imprisoned
by our ideals, jumping like frenzied
apes rattling the bars of their cage.

Be a fool! Benevolence and peace
are only for fools. An order of some kind
will come to settle over your heart
like scum in a riverbed.

Be a fool! If you are slandered, don't whimper.
You cannot win, but you won't be a loser.
Be as idiotic as death will be, at last.

This way you will never speak a false word,
you will be calm, collected, strong, and free—
a welcome tableguest in future and past.

## I Did Not Know

I always believed theories of guilt
were only fairy tales, to be laughed at,
stupid, lame raps—you talk about guilt
when you're afraid to act!

I did not know that so many horrors
hid in the chambers of my heart.
I thought it offered dreams with every beat
like a mother rocking her child to sleep.

Now I know better. This great truth sheds light
on the original infamy in my heart
shining like a sleek black coffin.

And my mouth would have groaned out on its own
(had I not spoken): so I would not be all alone,
why can't you all be as guilty as I am?

# GUILT

I think I am a hardened sinner
    although I feel all right.
Only one trifle bothers me:
    Guilty, yes—but of what?

There is no doubt about my guilt.
    But no matter how I rack my brain
I cannot point out my crime.
    Maybe it is simple and plain.

Like a miser after his vanished gold
    I rummage for this sin.
I have abandoned my mother for its sake
    although my heart is not made of tin.

Some day I'll find it, you'll see,
    among the champions of morality.
Then I will have to confess
    and invite my friends for tea.

I'll tell them I have killed. Whom,
    I am not sure. Perhaps my father.
I looked on while he bled away
    as night congealed into day.

I stabbed him with a knife. I won't
    elaborate, we are all mortal—
and any day, like someone stabbed,
    suddenly any one of us may fall.

I'll tell all, then wait to see
    who'll be too busy to stay
and who will fall into reverie
    and who will be horrified yet fay.

And then I shall notice the one
    whose eyes signal, warm:
There are others here like you, son,
    you are not the only one . . .

But possibly my guilt is childish
    and really dumb.
Then the size of the world will diminish
    and I will let it play on.

I don't believe in god; if one exists,
    no need to bother with me.
I shall absolve myself, and the living
    will help set me free.

# A Breath Of Air!

Who can forbid my telling what hurt me
    on the way home?
Soft darkness was just settling on the grass,
    a velvet drizzle,
and under my feet the brittle leaves
tossed sleeplessly and moaned
    like beaten children.

Stealthy shrubs were squatting in a circle
    on the city's outskirts.
The autumn wind cautiously stumbled among them.
    The cool moist soil
looked with suspicion at streetlamps;
a wild duck woke clucking in a pond
    as I walked by.

I was thinking, anyone could attack me
    in that lonely place.
Suddenly a man appeared,
    but walked on.
I watched him go. He could have robbed me,
since I wasn't in the mood for self-defence.
    I felt crippled.

They can tap all my telephone calls
    (when, why, to whom.)
They have a file on my dreams and plans
    and on those who read them.
And who knows when they'll find
sufficient reason to dig up the files
    that violate my rights.

In this country, fragile villages
    —where my mother was born—
have fallen from the tree of living rights
    like these leaves
and when a full-grown misery treads on them
a small noise reports their misfortune
    as they're crushed alive.

This is not the order I dreamed of. My soul
     is not at home here
in a world where the insidious
     vegetate easier,
among people who dread to choose
and tell lies with averted eyes
     and feast when someone dies.

This is not how I imagined order.
     Even though
I was beaten as a small child, mostly
     for no reason,
I would have jumped at a single kind word.
I knew my mother and my kin were far,
     these people were strangers.

Now I have grown up. There is more foreign
     matter in my teeth,
more death in my heart. But I still have rights
     until I fall apart
into dust and soul, and now that I've grown up
my skin is not so precious that I should put up
     with the loss of my freedom.

My leader is in my heart. We are
     men, not beasts,
we have minds. While our hearts ripen desires,
     they cannot be kept in files.
Come, freedom! Give birth to a new order,
teach me with good words and let me play,
     your beautiful serene son.

## BELATED LAMENT

Mother, my fever is ninety-eight point six,
and you are not here to take care of me.
Instead, like an easy woman, when called,
you stretched out by death's side.
I try to piece you together from soft
autumn landscapes and women dear to me,
but I can see there won't be time.
This fire is burning me away.

It was the end of the war
when I went to the country that last time.
In the city, all the stores were empty—
no food, not even bread.
I lay flat on my belly on top of a boxcar
to bring you flour and potatoes in a sack.
I, your stubborn son, brought a chicken for you.
But you weren't there.

You took yourself and your sweet breasts
from me and gave them to maggots.
The words you used to scold, to comfort
were nothing but cheating, lying words.
You cooled my bowl of soup, you stirred it,
'Eat, my baby, grow tall for me.'
Now your empty mouth bites into damp and grease
—o you have deceived me.

I should have devoured you! You gave your own
dinner, but did I ask for it? And why did you
break your back doing all that laundry?
So that the coffin might straighten it out?
I would be glad to have you beat me once more.
I'd be happy, because I could hit you back.
You are worthless! You just want to be dead!
You spoil everything! You are a ghost!

You are a greater cheat than any woman
that ever deceived me. You wailed,
you gave birth out of love,

—and then you stole away.
O you gipsy, you wheedled, you gave
only to steal it back in the last hour.
Your child wants to swear and curse—
mother, can't you hear? Stop me!

Slowly the mind calms down,
the myths run out.
The child who clings to his mother's love
sees how foolish he has been.
Every mother's son is let down in the end,
either deceived, or else trying to cheat.
You can try to fight, and you'll be killed.
Or else make your peace—and die.

## When The Moon Shines

When the moon shines, in my dreams a mute
otherworldly light floods the halls.
A child sneaks into the kitchen, to cut
bread and quickly stuff it in his mouth.

Only the drafts know him in the sleeping house.
His knees shake, scared big eyes stare hard,
while his hand rummages like a mouse
among milk jugs and containers of lard.

The terrible cupboard keeps creaking:
the boy's hand freezes at his mouth.
He'd beg for mercy but silence, that unforgiving
cruel loudspeaker, magnifies the sound.

The noise (cosmic creaking), the strife,
instead of stopping, grows and rages on.
The child turns pale. He drops the knife
and sneaks back to lie down . . .

When I wake up the sun flames, ice melts,
everywhere clumsy shards scattered—
like plateglass from an exotic fruit display
that the clenched fist of hunger shattered.

Heaven relents, the frost god fades away.
Tired of hell, the devil tries a new game,
and directs his lush heat our way:
trees and shrubs break out in green flame.

# ON FREUD'S EIGHTIETH BIRTHDAY

What you hide in your heart
open up for your eyes
and await in your heart
what you foresee with your eyes.

They say that love leads
the living toward death.
Yet we crave pleasure
as we crave bread.

And all who live are children
longing for their mother's lap.
When not embracing, they're killing—
the battlefield is a marriage bed.

May you be like the Old One,
mauled by the young,
who, bleeding away,
sires a million sons.

The thorn that once stuck in your foot
has now fallen out.
And now even your death
drops quietly from your heart.

Let your hands fill
with what your eyes see ahead.
Either kiss or kill
the one you hide in your heart.

## BY THE DANUBE

1

Sitting on the steps of the quay
I watched a melon rind floating away.
Submerged in my fate I barely heard
the surface chatter. From the depths: not a word.
And just like my heart's high tide
the Danube was murky, wise, wide.

Like muscles at work, muscles that
make bricks, dig, hammer and hoe—
that's how each movement of each wave
kicked into action, tensed and let go.
The river, like mother, told tales, lulled me,
and washed the city's dirty laundry.

A slow drizzle began to fall, but soon
gave up, as if it were all the same.
Still, I watched the horizon like one
inside a cave, watching a steady rain:
this gray eternal rain pouring, steadfast,
so transparent now, the many-colored past.

The Danube flowed on.  Small white-
crested waves played laughing my way
like children in the lap of a fertile
young mother who sits dreaming away.
Awash in time's flood they chattered,
so many headstones, graveyards shattered.

2

With me, it takes one hundred thousand years
looking on so I can suddenly see
in a flash, all of time's totality—
and ten thousand ancestors look on with me.

I can see what they could not, being too busy
plowing, killing, loving, doing what they had to do.

And they, having settled back into matter, can see
what I cannot, when I must testify for you.

We know each other as joy knows sorrow.
The past is mine, theirs the present.
We write this poem—when they touch my pen
I start to remember, feeling their presence.


3


My mother was Kuman, my father half Székely
and half, perhaps all, Romanian.
Food tasted sweeter from my mother's mouth,
from father's came the beauty of truth.
Each move I make, it's their embrace.
At times it makes me sad—this death,
this is how I was made. They call to me. "Son,
you'll see, when we are gone . . ."

They speak to me, through me, become me;
being weak this is how I grow strong,
reminded I am more than a throng:
I am each ancestor, back to the first cell,
the First One that split and multiplied.
Turned into mother and father, I glow—
and father, mother each divide in two,
and I expand into One vast soul.

I am the world—all that once was is still alive,
today it is still tribe against tribe.
Long-gone conquerors are my living dead,
I suffer the torments of the defeated.
Settler and exile, lawmaker and rebel,
Turk, Tatar, Romanian, Slovak—today's
Hungarians!—all swirl in my heart:
we owe a gentle future to the past!

. . . I want to work. This was strife enough,
having to own up to the past
by the Danube, whose gentle waves
embrace past, present and tomorrow.

The battles our ancestors had to fight
resolve into peace in remembrance's light.
It is time to work together at last
on our affairs in common—no small task.

## As In A Field

As in a field a storm
overtaking a small boy,
no other: mother or farmhouse to run for
on churning feet,
the sky is thick with angry rumble,
a single straw swirls in the stubble,
animal-like he whimpers,
would sob, but his fears
have robbed his warm tears,
would sigh
but now the sky
exhales cold breath
suddenly at his thin
body and face, lit
by a pale shiver-like lightning
and black rain falls pouring
as if he were the source
of tears beyond measure
pooling in the fields
washing bright verdure,
digging the pit, flooding the hollow,
sweeping over brook and meadow,
in the air a swooping shadow,
as the boy sets out on his way
that's his through time and space—
that's how fierce the sudden rage
of desire that swept me so
I cried forgetting my age
and on this tearsoaked soil
that makes your feet so heavy
even as you would like to hurry—
I stop and stand now. If she loved me,
I wouldn't even notice this desire.

## It Hurts A Lot

Inside, outside
death stalks your hide
(scared little mouse, run for your hole)—

as long as you yearn
you'll keep running to her
for sheltering arms, knees, her whole

being, lured there
by her warm lap and desire;
you are thrown there by your need—

and so all who find
woman's embrace, cling and grind
until their lips turn white with greed.

Twofold guerdon,
twofold treasure, this love-burden.
He who loves and finds no other

is as homeless
as a wild beast, and as helpless:
an animal in need, sans shelter.

You will find no
other refuge, even if you
dare point the knife at your mother!

There was one who had heard
the meaning of my words
but still thrust me away from her.

And so, ever since,
I have no place in life. My head spins,
a patchwork of cares and aches

like a small boy
and his rattle, the toy
only the lonely child shakes.

What should I do
against, or for her: fight or woo?
It's no shame to find out, it seems,

since the world will
thrust out and kill
the sun-dazed, terrorized by dreams.

I drop away
"culture" like clothes that stay
thrown by carefree lovers on the ground.

Where does it say
that I should suffer alone this way
while she watches death slapping me around?

Newborns suffer
given birth by the mother.
But the pain is eased by sharing.

As for me, my
painful song brings only money,
followed by more shame and agony.

Help me! Small boys,
let your eyes burst
when she walks by.

Innocent babes,
under bootheels scream out, please,
cry, let her know: it hurts a lot.

Faithful old dogs
get run over by the machine's cogs,
howl out to her: it hurts a lot!

Pregnant women
abort your burden,
cry out to her: it hurts a lot!

Healthy humans,
fall down, get crushed,
groan out to her: it hurts a lot.

All you men who
claw each other for a woman,
do not hold back: it hurts a lot.

Stallions, bulls
gelded for the yoke to pull,
bellow at her: it hurts a lot.

Oh you mute fish
bite the hook, thrash,
gape up at her: it hurts a lot.

All things living,
in pain quivering,
in woods and field, let your homes burn

till you've gathered
your charred flesh around her bed
and moan with me: it hurts a lot.

All her life long
let her hear it, she has done wrong,
on a sheer whim she has denied

the last refuge
inside, outside
for a man who's trying to hide.

# FIREWOOD

The freight station bridge still trembles
and a fussy autumn wind purrs around
the boxcar rumbling with the sound
of split firewood being thrown down.

A piece may shift, but the fallen heap lies
mute . . . What ails me? Afraid to look back,
running with split firewood in a sack:
the boy I once was is still here.

The little kid I was is still around
and the grownup may be choked by regret,
but no tears: he hums his song,
making sure he hangs on to his hat.

Was it you I feared, tough-looking men
I admired as you tossed the wood?
I still carry you around, stolen firewood
in this homeless world full of guards.

FLORA

1.

*Hexameters*

Crumbling slush and snow, leaky tin gutter starting its
drip-drop, in heaps that turned black, the ice faints away,
evanesces, is gone, juices gush forth and cavort twittering, a
foamy flood toward sewers. Fleeting, this lissome sunlight,
making the heavenly highness quiver and happy desire flings
her shirt blushing on dawn's landscape.

Fearful, reviving, can you see how much I love you, Flora?
In this beautiful chattering spring thaw the grief from my
heart,
like a bandage from a wound, you have lifted—again I'm a-
tingle.
Your eternal name's flood calls, fragile, sweet sunshine,
makes me shiver seeing I have lived so long without you.

2.

*Mysteries*

Mysteries are calling me:
stand awake in a fairytale.
You wrapped me up, and made me wear
this heavy faith, like chain mail.

Singing water, singing breeze,
you'll blush when you'll understand.
Singing eyes and singing heart
go all out to win your hand.

So I'm writing you a song:
'long as I'm bound to love you—
help me lighten up this load,
this heavy faith I owe you.

## FOR FLORA

I feel compelled to muse about what
I would do if you loved me not:
I could then put out my costly fires,
I could then shut my tired eyes.

For it is good to die. Perhaps I'd be glad
if you did not love me so. I would sit
there under white-foamed green skies,
next to pattering clouds of stars

out there on the shores of tranquility,
on the banks of space that is not empty,
to look on and contemplate worlds
as you would flowers on a tree.

One summer when I was a ship's boy
on a clattering tugboat named Tatar,
one beautiful idle summer day,
as if studying how to be happy,

I stared at the Danube: its high flood
brought branches in full leaf, afloat,
and so many ruffling wavelets alive,
all nibbling at planks awash in the tide,

and all those beautiful melons, flashes
in the yellow flood, you would not believe,
nor would I perhaps, if
I were not telling you all this.

There came also red apples bobbing,
and green peppers swam by, swaying,
each moment something new for the eye.
Rocking and dipping, the boat stood by.

This is what viewing space would be like.
Nodding at each new thing, "How lovely!"
I would then be able to judge how blue
is the celestial blue suited to you.

For the cosmos is our free gift
into the bargain. Life's flash flood
inundates past the shorelines of death,
past hearts and spaces and their depths,

way past the silent borderline
just like the Danube that summertime . . .
Because you love me and I can sleep in peace,
to you I might as well confess

that, caught in the act by transitoriness,
I, too, was unable to contain myself:
that's why my soul is now public property,
and that's why I love you so deeply.

## MARCH, 1937

I

Mild, misty rain drizzles on
downy young spring wheat in bud.
The stork returns to the chimney,
beaten winter to the icy north.
Green explosions announce
the merry vernal violence.
In front of a carpenter's shop
fresh pine scent gives a whiff of hope.

What's in the news? In Spain
the gang ravages and rages;
in China a dumb general chases
peasants from their few small
acres. Armies bark threats,
clean linen soaks in blood.
The poor are tormented.
War-mongerers rattle about.

I am happy. My soul is a child;
Flora loves me. But we are doomed:
against our naked beautiful love
heavy metal tanks are sent out
by the vilest men. I am alarmed
by the zealousness of this scum.
Only in ourselves do I find comfort
and life-strength to carry on.

II

Mercenary man and his paid slut—
their hearts I am unable to touch.
Their evil may be overamplified
yet I still fear for my life,
for I have nothing else beside.
But the watchful mind has thought ahead.
If violated Earth grows cold,
Flora, my heart's love will still glow.

For we shall create a lovely, bright girl
and a brave, understanding manchild
who will save of us some shred
—as sunlight in the Milky Way reflected—
so that even when the Sun wanes,
our offspring will fly full of faith
in their fine craft, as it soars
to cultivate the stars.

## BIRTHDAY POEM

So—I lived to be thirty-two!
This poem is a surprise, too:
    itty-
      bitty

gift that came my way
in a corner of this café,
    from me
      to me.

My thirty-two years have flown,
never had two hundred a month of my own.
    That's right,
      some birthright!

I could have been a college teacher
instead of an idle pen-pusher,
    boho
    hobo.

But at the university in Szeged
I was summarily expelled
    by a mean
    dean.

His reproof came quick and hard,
for my poem "With a Pure Heart"—
    he'd defend
    the homeland

against me with drawn sword.
And so my spirit's conjured
    his name,
    and fame:

"You sir, as long as I'm competent,
will not teach on this continent,"
    he blustered,
    flustered.

But Professor Horger, if it gives you cheer
that this poet is not a grammar teacher,
    control
    your joy—

I shall instruct a whole nation,
not only the high-school population,
    you'll see,
    you'll see.

## AN ANCIENT RAT

An ancient rat spreads disease among us:
unconsidered, un-thought-out thought,
sniffing into what we have cooked up,
running from human to human, caught.
It makes the drunkard unaware
that drowning his mood in champagne
he's swilling down the meager fare
of some starving family in pain.

And since the spirit of nations cannot
express the fresh juice of human rights,
you see new kinds of ethnic infamies
stir humankind against humankind.
Oppression descends in crowing flocks
upon living hearts as on carrion
and misery trickles over the globe
like saliva from an idiot's chin.

Summers pinned down by starvation droop
their wings in misery's glass case.
All over our souls machines crawl
like vermin over a sleeper's face.
We hide faith and gratitude deep
within, shed tears onto flames.
We thirst revenge, only to keep
succumbing to conscience's games.

And like a jackal that turns to the sky
to disgorge its howling at the stars,
it is at heaven where agonies shine
that the poet sends up his bootless cries . . .
Oh you constellations! So many rusty
rapacious iron daggers all around
stabbing my soul over and over—
(around here only death gains ground).

Still, I have faith. My eyes filled with tears,
I beseech you, future, be less fierce . . .
I have faith, for unlike our forebears
today we are no longer drawn and quartered.

Some day the peace of freedom will arrive
and torments will become more rarefied,
until we, too, will be forgotten at last
in arbors where gentle shadows are cast.

## Long Ago

Long ago I realized
I'm amphibious like a frog
that lies low at the bottom
of raging skies. This poem
is a bubble of my anxious soul.

I have no evil masters and
no worms await my command.
Like fish and gods I survive
in oceans and heavens alike.

My ocean is the murky world
of gentle, warm embracing arms.
My heaven is the clear light
of humanity conceived by the mind.

## WHEN YOUR SOUL

When your soul and mind
flow babbling through
things and skies
like a brook over rocks—

high on your heart's flood
you may suddenly know it:
you don't need another's lines,
you are the poet!

In my garden
the tobacco leaf ripens.
The lyric has its logic
but it's not a science.

# At Last I Understand My Father

At last I understand my father,
who, across the resounding ocean,
had set out for America.

He'd gone away, it's nothing new,
to bravely collar the good fortune
that was by rights his due.

His chances dwindled, his hope
embittered, in the old country
he was tired of boiling scented soap.

At last I understand my father,
who, across the wavering ocean,
had set out for America.

While the gentlemen filibustered,
he packed his bag and moved on where
hard work earned good money, he'd heard.

In the forests back home not a leaf was his,
all the way over he remembered—
and threw up on the heaving waves.

Wisely, he had left his family.
His children shouldn't have to bless him
for each meager hard-earned penny—

only to curse him after he dies.
No, he was not a preacher of morals,
nor was he loyal to clouds of lies.

At last I understand my father,
who, across the deceptive ocean,
had set out for America.

At last, as I set out for my
New World: Flora is my America.
Slowly, the old coastlines sink and die,

I'm no longer lost in those pains and fears.
From the depths of human faces
an edge of new understanding appears.

Just like my father had set out—
even if God never existed,
I would still trust this world to God.

This is not shrinking from the fight:
for love, I would cheat and kill—
but in acceptable ways, if you will.

## I SAW BEAUTY

I saw beauty, sweetness:
I imagined a frail rose.
And reality, as I stared,
crashed rock-like against my head.

But this rock is a metaphor.
It is best if I speak plainly.
That's what I'm taught by cares'
instructive daily duty.

My intuition was right
as soon as the man came in.
"He's here to turn off the power."
My head roared like an ocean.

The knife lay on the table,
ready for pencil sharpening.
To stab him would have meant
getting even for everything.

I was in despair that now
all would be dark and sad.
Animals may defend their lair
but ours is a different war.

Resorting to arms is weakness:
the enemy kills and conquers
by driving away one's sweetness.
Money is king of law and order.

Warfare these days is a different notion.
The hero never draws the sword.
Banknotes set off each explosion,
scattering shrapnel, pieces of gold.

Thus reasoning, I said goodnight
and turned in toward the wall.
Later I woke to the light
of smiling stars. The moon was full.

## DUSK

This sharp, clear dusk was made for me.
Far off, bare branches construct
delicate support for empty air.
The self, made subject, separates from the world,
becomes self-absorbed, perhaps destroyed.
Who knows? Intuition could give the answer,
but, like a dog scolded by its master,
it wanders morosely in the frozen yard,
howling at strangers. It will not speak,
and without it, what am I to do?
One thing is sure here—there's been a mistake.
It's good that iambs still exist: something
to hang on to. This is how children learn to walk.
But I cannot be a child, because I am
too fretful, stubborn, treacherous . . .
Perhaps because all humans are just as
sly and pigheaded. Are they? I cannot tell.
One winks at me and says, "You lovely man,"
the other goes, "Lazy slob, you're not working again,
but you make sure your belly's full." (Perhaps
I shouldn't?) This one shoves money in my hand,
"Be happy, I, too, have suffered, I understand."
Another would steal even the pillow under my head.
I'm jerked around, handled, jostled, croaked at,
yet no one notices this hunchback I lug around
like a crazed mother the fetus in her womb,
to give birth to silence, pure emptiness in a room.

## You Brought a Stake

You brought a sharp stake, not a flower,
you argued, in this world, with the other,
promised a bag of gold to your mother,
and look where you are slumped now:

like some toadstool by a treestump
(you need to be cared for, you chump)
imprisoned at the Seven Towers—
you'll never escape from this dump.

Babyteeth against stone: why bite?
Why hurry, to be left behind?
Why didn't you dream at night?
What was it you wanted in the end?

You always left yourself unsheltered,
your wounds you constantly picked at,
you're famous now, is that what you wanted?
So what else is new, you idiot?

So you have loved? Who clung to you?
You went into exile? Who banished you?
Own it all up, else it will own you.
You have no knife here and no bread.

Here at the Seven Towers, imprisoned,
be glad if you have enough firewood,
be glad if your bed is cushioned.
Lay down your head, and be good.

## Here, At Last, I Found My Home

I finally found my home,
the land where my name
is correctly spelled above the grave
where I'm buried—if I'm buried.

This earth will take me in
like an alms box.
No one wants a worthless coin
left over from the days of war,

or the iron ring engraved with
the fine words: new world, rights,
land. Our laws are still for war
and gold rings are preferred.

I was alone for a long time.
Then many came to visit me.
'You live alone' they said, though
gladly I would have lived among them.

That's how I lived, in vain,
I'll be the first to say.
They made me play the fool.
Now even my death is useless.

While I lived, I tried
to stand up against the whirlwind.
The joke is, I harmed less
than I was harmed.

Spring is fine, and so is summer,
but autumn's better, and winter's best
for one who finally leaves his hopes
for a family and a home to others.

## ONLY YOU SHOULD READ MY POEMS

Only you should read my poems
who know me and love me well,
since you sail in nothingness,
and, like a prophet, can foretell

the future, for silence in your dreams
has taken on a human form
and in your heart at times appear
the tiger and the gentle deer.